JOURNEYS

Young Readers' Letters to Authors Who Changed Their Lives

Shaw Island School
44 Hoffman Cove Road
Shaw Island, WA 98286

JOURNEYS

YOUNG READERS' LETTERS TO AUTHORS WHO CHANGED THEIR LIVES

LIBRARY OF CONGRESS CENTER FOR THE BOOK

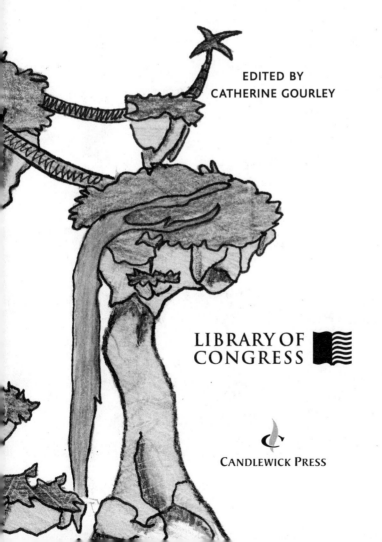

EDITED BY
CATHERINE GOURLEY

LIBRARY OF
CONGRESS

CANDLEWICK PRESS

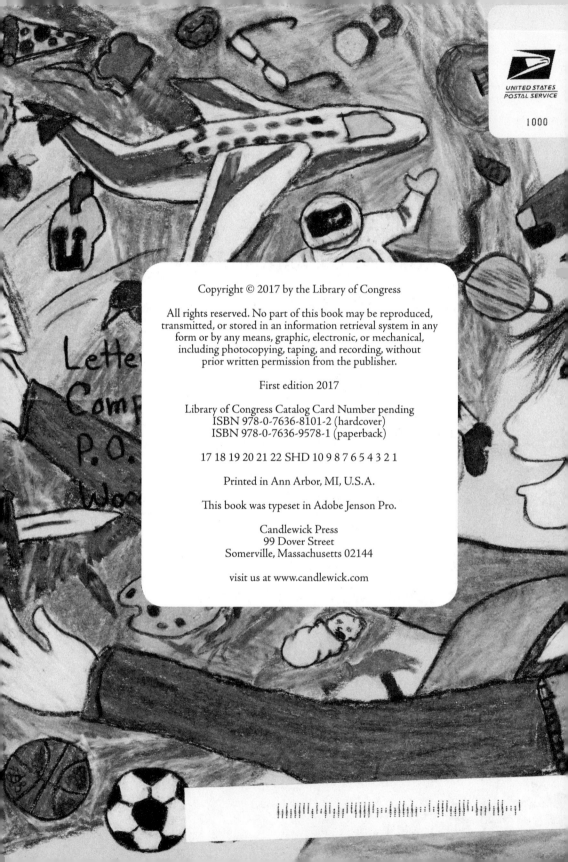

First edition 2017

Library of Congress Catalog Card Number pending
ISBN 978-0-7636-8101-2 (hardcover)
ISBN 978-0-7636-9578-1 (paperback)

17 18 19 20 21 22 SHD 10 9 8 7 6 5 4 3 2 1

Printed in Ann Arbor, MI, U.S.A.

This book was typeset in Adobe Jenson Pro.

Candlewick Press
99 Dover Street
Somerville, Massachusetts 02144

visit us at www.candlewick.com

CONTENTS

FOREWORD by John Y. Cole xi

PREFACE xiii

• PART ONE •

Upper Elementary: Finding a Friend, Finding a Voice

CHAPTER ONE: DESTINATIONS

"My life is so different from yours." • Alessandra Selassie 3

"I wanted to jump into the story and yell." • Hanna Lee 8

"I became Crispin, living in the Middle Ages." • Thomas J. Cienki 11

"Your poem is my winter." • Katja Saana Sinikka Martin 13

CHAPTER TWO: REALIZATIONS

"It's true. Nobody wants to talk to nobodies." • Erica Langan 15

"I used to find it hard to forgive my dad." • Taaja Immani Draughn 18

"The only person who didn't understand anything was me."
Jayanth Uppaluri 21

"I can hide from being Jewish. You couldn't." • Eliana Kahn 26

"In my opinion, diversity is a good thing." • Chelsea Brown 29

"When it seems like I'm all alone, I'm really not."
Lacie Craven Glidden 32

"Mushy answers don't feel true." • Darius Atefat-Peckham   35

"Life is a big stinking blob of mess." • Gerel Sanzhikov   39

"Maybe your words weren't meant just for me." • Anna Mytko   43

CHAPTER THREE: RETURNING HOME

"The spiraling piece of lead had shattered my heart."
Linnea Rain Lentfer   46

"I have not done anything dangerous or illegal." • Davis Klimek   48

"The Keep pile, the Throw Out pile, and the Keep in the Attic pile"
Becky Miller   51

"In the future it will be my turn to carry on what my grandparents
and parents have fought for." • Aleema Kelly   55

"Even in a sea of clovers, flowers find each other." • Hillary V. Schiff   58

• PART TWO •
MIDDLE SCHOOL: A NEW AWARENESS

CHAPTER FOUR: DESTINATIONS

"I left my world behind and entered a new one." • Janet Lynne Snow   63

"I found myself raising my butterbeer mug to that brave
Boy Who Lived." Anne Overton   66

"To my surprise, your book was a great inspiration to me — not boring at all." • Abbie Beaver   71

"Queen of Up, Up" • Arielle Moosman   75

CHAPTER FIVE: REALIZATIONS

"Because, dearest Anne, because your Kitty understands." • Jisoo Choi   79

"For the first time in my life, I found a part of the German nation with which I could sympathize." • Bertina Kudrin   83

"All students learn differently." • Jonathan Hoff   87

"I felt a twinge of fear at what I could become." • Kara S. Moritz   91

"Keeping a leash on the minds of school-age children"
Shannon Chinn   95

"For the first time, I heard my own silence." • Emmy Goyette   100

"It was uncomfortable to look into his world and see the pain."
Gabriel Ferris   104

CHAPTER SIX: RETURNING HOME

"I still imagine my bedroom as a hobbit-hole." • Elizabeth Chambers 108

"Gone was the ice skater; gone were the Olympics." • Ellie Ball   113

"It was a hate crime." • Margaret Veglahn   117

"I saw my brother Joe try to fight death." • Juliana Gorman   121

"I'm pressing play." • Bailee Stump   126

• PART THREE •
HIGH SCHOOL: "I AM NOT A NOBODY"

CHAPTER SEVEN: DESTINATIONS

"Courage to conquer my fears" • Anna Marie Wichorek 133

"I became lost in the Kabul of Amir's childhood." • Audrey 137

"I no longer hide in my flannel sheets, waiting for my problems
to disappear." • Gabrielle Sclafani 142

CHAPTER EIGHT: REALIZATIONS

"I was weighed down, coated in a layer of plastic." • Emily Waller 147

"It is difficult to reconcile my hate and my love."
Hannah DesChamp 151

"Words seemed weak and cruelly useless." • Alexandra McLaughlin 155

"My mother was my salvation from my father." • Joshua Tiprigan 160

"The judgmental, racist, hateful monster I feared was myself."
Xiomara Torres 164

"My mother sits at her corner in the East, and I at the West."
Ayesha Usmani 168

"I, too, take advantage of my mother." • Lisa Le 172

"I needed to please everyone and have everyone pleased with me."
Kelsey Bowen 176

"In order to protect ourselves, we have to hurt our loved ones."
Macoy Churchill 180

CHAPTER NINE: RETURNING HOME

"I am not fat anymore. I never was, I suppose." · Julia Mueller   184

"You didn't even try." · Abby Swegarden   188

"I am armed with your words." · Aidan Kingwell   193

"This is a city in need of a Holden Caulfield." · Martha Park   198

"You were so unspeakably right." · Devi Acharya   201

"I consider writing another form of resistance."
   Annie Schnitzer   205

LEGACY   209

ABOUT THE CENTER FOR THE BOOK   211

SOURCE NOTES   212

BIBLIOGRAPHY   218

INDEX   225

Thomas Jefferson, America's founding father and third president, understood the power of words, not just to inform but also to inspire. In a letter to John Adams, he wrote, "I cannot live without books." Nor did Jefferson believe his new country and its citizens could live without a library. Established in 1800, the Library of Congress is the world's largest library and uniquely American, reflecting this country's cultural nationalism.

The Center for the Book in the Library of Congress fulfills Thomas Jefferson's philosophy of promoting libraries and the development of lifelong readers through programs that celebrate our country's literary diversity and leadership. Letters About Literature is one of the Center's most popular reading promotion programs for young people.

The Center's own "journey" with Letters About Literature began in 1984 with a program called "Books Make a Difference," an annual essay-writing contest cosponsored by Weekly Reader. Over time, the program grew into the more personal venue of letter writing — something Thomas Jefferson, too, would appreciate. He spent hours each day writing correspondence, what he called his "pen and ink" work.

Over the years that Letters About Literature has invited young readers to share their personal responses to authors with us at the Center for the Book, we have learned that children often approach reading with reluctance and that writing about what they read is often a challenge and, for some, a struggle.

This volume of letters is a showcase of young minds and hearts inspired and at times healed by the power of an author's words. As the letters so poignantly illustrate, not all books are right for all readers. Likewise, two readers can interpret and respond to the same book quite differently. For some children, finding that right author, that right book, is in itself a bit of a journey. Once a reader finds that author and that book, something remarkable occurs. Readers discover themselves within the pages of the book. They begin to feel and to understand.

Each year, thousands of young readers send us their letters. Their "pen and ink" work is personal and thoughtful and sincere. Thomas Jefferson would be proud of these young readers — not simply because they read books, but because they think about the books they read.

John Y. Cole, Director and Founder
The Center for the Book in the Library of Congress

• PREFACE •

In a letter to author Veronica Roth, a young reader writes, "Books can take you places, places that don't exist but come to life because we all have imagination. You meet the characters, you get inside their heads, know what they're thinking. And then you get attached to them. They worm their way into your heart and they don't budge. That's how I know I'm reading a great book."

This book is an atlas through some young readers' literary journeys, as told in the letters they've written to authors living or dead, whose works have touched them in very personal ways.

For twenty-five years, the Letters About Literature competition, promoted by the Center for the Book in the Library of Congress, has challenged readers in grades four through twelve to explore how books have changed their view of their world or themselves. It's the Center for the Book's most popular national reading program to promote reading among young people.

But why letters? Why do so many twenty-first-century young readers, all of whom are expert at texting and tweeting and social mediating, willingly revert to such an old-fashioned form of communication?

A letter is not abstract or virtual. Like those other forms of communication, it travels through space and time, but oh so much more slowly. That slowness is sweetness. There's an anticipation for the writer, sending it off, wondering if it has arrived yet. And then there's an anticipation for the recipient, opening the envelope and unfolding the paper. The reader can touch it and perhaps even sense the presence of the writer who formed the words. Letters can be history. Letters, tied in bundles and saved in drawers, have so often been stepping-stones for readers that span decades, even centuries!

A letter is far more private than a status update on a social network. With the private comes the personal, and because letters are so personal, they are insightful. In their letters to authors, the young people represented in this collection tell us what they value and desire as well as what they fear or dread.

Like a drawer of saved letters, this collection is arranged in bundles. Here, the bundles are grouped by upper elementary, middle-school, and high-school letter writers, and, within each of those categories, further grouped by the stages of a journey: destination, realization, and the return home. The title for each passage is a phrase taken from the young reader's letter. Each letter is introduced with a short passage about the author and the work about which the reader has written. The letters have been minimally edited so as not to interfere with the writer's voice.

Journeys is not about lessons learned. Rather, it is a travel catalog of sometimes exciting, sometimes emotional destinations to which young readers book passage. It illustrates, often poignantly, how reading can take us away from the present and bring us back home again, transformed with new insight into ourselves and our world.

· PART ONE ·
UPPER ELEMENTARY

Finding a Friend, Finding a Voice

"When journeying to Elsewhere, Jonas found bits of joy in the colorful blue sky, a sweet scented flower, or the throaty warble of a new bird. *The Giver* showed me that even simple things in life are beautiful, such as the rich smell of a chocolate bar or the bright yellow of a leaf in fall. . . . It's amazing how much a novel that is well written can affect a person. It will not only change the way you think, but if it is good enough, it can change the way you act."

—Lucy Dyal in a letter to Lois Lowry
about her book *The Giver*

The Long Winter
Laura Ingalls Wilder

"My life is so different from yours."
Alessandra Selassie

"These times are too progressive. Everything has changed too fast. Railroads and telegraph and kerosene and coal stoves — they're good to have but the trouble is, folks get to depend on 'em."

So says Pa in Laura Ingalls Wilder's *The Long Winter*, the sixth book of her Little House series, based on her own childhood on the American frontier in the late nineteenth century. Born in 1867 near Pepin, Wisconsin, Laura moved with her family farther westward when she was not quite two years old. Pa and Ma settled for a time in Kansas, then moved once again to Minnesota, and eventually to the Dakota Territory. Laura attended school infrequently. Still, she and her sisters taught themselves, as many pioneering families did during this time. In 1882, Laura received her teaching certificate.

Not until the 1920s, when she was much older, did she begin to write about her childhood. *The Long Winter* was published in 1940, sixty years after the winter in which one blizzard followed another, almost burying the Wilder cabin. In the eight decades since its publication, countless readers have traveled back in time to experience through Wilder's vivid details what life was like for a young girl growing up on the edge of the wilderness.

Dear Laura Ingalls Wilder,

My life could not be more different from your life and the lives of the pioneers that you describe in your series of books. I live in the American capital, Washington, D.C., and enjoy all the things modern life has to offer. I have a Safeway around the corner and don't have to worry about growing my own food. When I want to go somewhere, I go by car, or if it's far, I go by plane, which gets me there quickly and safely. When I want water, I turn on the tap. When it's dark, I turn on a light. While my life is so different from yours, I was still so touched by your books because they helped me to finally understand the life of someone I love: my father.

My dad grew up in Eritrea, in Africa. It was a new country, and he and his family were part of building the nation, just as your family was part of building America. My dad often jokes that his mom made sure that they weren't picky eaters by not giving them much to eat. It's hard for me to imagine not having enough to eat. If we run out of food, we go to the store, but your book *The Long Winter* really made me understand what it must feel like to worry about not having enough. I saw in the way Pa and Ma worried about feeding their children how hard it must have been for my grandma and grandpa with their six children. My father also talks about meeting his friends at night to study under the light of one of the few street lamps in the town. You studied by the light of an oil lamp, and Pa and Ma worried about having enough money to buy oil for it.

When I read about your dolls made out of scraps of fabric, it made me think about my dad's stories of making a ball out of a sock filled with old clothing and scraps of fabric. We feel sad today to hear of kids having so little, but when you describe your childhood and to hear my dad's stories, I realize what good childhoods you both had. You both didn't have many toys, but you made up games and created your own fun.

Even though my dad grew up in a different place and time from pioneer America, when I was reading your books I realized how similar your lives were in terms of the way people interacted. Children had to respect their elders. They didn't talk back like characters on TV do today. Children were expected to do a lot of chores and help take care of the family house. I have a couple of chores to do, but nothing like what my father had to do. He was the eldest, so he had to take care of his younger siblings. His mom didn't hire a babysitter like you would today. The way he played with siblings and friends wasn't over Wii, or playing computer games, or talking through Instagram or Facebook, or anything with technology. They got together, face-to-face, and played with each other, ran around outside, explored nature, or told each other stories and jokes. I can see how this would make a stronger relationship than wanting to kill each other on a Wii game! As much as I love technology, it sounds like fun going back to these kinds of friendships. Today, we think people are important because they have money or are famous. In Eritrea and in pioneer times, it didn't matter how much you had. It wasn't cool to be rude or to have a snappy comeback. You didn't lie, because your word was very important. What mattered was being honorable.

In my dad's family, just like in your family, two things were really important: being self-reliant and getting an education. Knowing that you could grow your own food and support your family was important. People didn't have much, but they didn't want handouts. They wanted to work and work hard, just like your pa always did. I thought of my father when I read how Ma helped prepare you, Mary, and Carrie for school and how excited Ma and Pa were when you moved to a place that had a school. When my dad was five years old, his grandfather took him to register at school. His family had made sure he learned the alphabet before he went so that the school had to accept him even though he was younger than the normal age for starting school. I loved reading about how you all worked hard to make enough money to send Mary to the special school for the blind that was far away. My dad's parents worked hard to get him into a good high school that was also far away. This led to him finishing high school in America and then college and graduate school. Today, lots of kids complain about going to school, but you, Mary, and my dad always felt lucky to go.

Before reading your books, my dad would tell me stories about his childhood but I didn't really understand them. My life growing up in America is so different from his life was growing up in Eritrea. Also, he has lived in the United States so long that his life today is like almost any other American's. Reading your books, and having such a vivid image through a young girl's perspective, made me appreciate my dad's childhood and feel closer to him. It also showed me reasons behind many of his rules and his always emphasizing being honorable. This gave me a new way of looking at him and a new type of relationship with him. I know you wrote these books to help children understand the lives of American pioneers, but for me, it helped me see my father's African childhood as being less foreign. Thank you so much for writing this series.

Sincerely,

Alessandra Selassie

Firegirl
Tony Abbott

"I wanted to jump into the story and yell."
Hanna Lee

"A child who carries a book with a bookmark in it is in two places at the same time." So states a poster advertising a series of fantasy books written by Tony Abbott. His readers have a choice of many destinations — from the fantasy world of Droon to a version of fifth-century Britain that features flying reindeer. His award-winning contemporary novel *Firegirl* takes the reader into the awkward world of seventh grade, where physical appearances count and beauty makes you popular. The novel's main character, Tom, thinks of himself as fat and sweaty. But the new girl who arrives at school, who has been badly burned and requires skin grafts, teaches him about courage and self-confidence.

Dear Tony Abbott,

Were you ever the person standing alone in a corner? The last to get picked for a game? I was. What I wore, ate, and thought was completely different from my classmates.

Eyes that reflected everything in the minds of their owners shot disgusted glares at me. Everyone stayed away from me. Ignoring me. I didn't have any friends. I wanted to have friends like the other people. It always felt like my heart was an orange, filled with juice at first and then getting squeezed and squeezed until there was hardly any juicy happiness left inside.

This is the honest truth. When I first read your book *Firegirl*, I wasn't that interested. *It's just another story about some boy and there's probably going to be a girl that the boy likes and whatever.* That's what I thought. When the teacher said that Firegirl was a new student, I imagined a beautiful girl with long fiery hair, bright-red nails, large glowing eyes, and the other stuff that authors usually use to make fire as human as possible. How wrong I was. I couldn't believe that Firegirl was the person you made her to be. This was unlike any other story I have ever read.

From the moment Firegirl appeared, I was captured by the flowing words of your story. It felt like I was there with Tom when he watched his classmates make fun of Firegirl. I was furious at them. I couldn't believe that they would make fun of someone just because of what they looked like. I wanted to jump into the story and yell at them. I found myself arguing with the characters in the story and crying along with Firegirl. What other person would know better than me about being left out? I'm a person who gets kicked out of everything and then gets soccer balls thrown at me. Yet here was a person who matched my sufferings.

Firegirl seemed like my friend. We cried together and got glares together. I became oblivious to soccer-ball-throwing people. For the first time in a long time, I was happy. I had found a friend.

This book brought happiness to my life. I was found smiling and no longer self-pitying in the corner. I learned that although there was no one for me right now, there was always a friend for someone in the world. *Firegirl* taught me that no matter how mean other people are to you, if there is one person who is truly your friend, that is better than a million people who are half-friends. So now I say thank you for writing this book and for giving me a friend and, more important, hope.

Hanna Lee

Crispin: The Cross of Lead
Avi

"I became Crispin, living in the Middle Ages."
Thomas J. Cienki

"Good historical fiction reveals details of life in a given time period without beating the reader over the head with it," observes Jim Blasingame in an interview with Avi, who has been writing historical novels for more than four decades. In his Newbery Medal–winning novel *Crispin: The Cross of Lead*, Avi weaves "fact and incident" seamlessly six centuries into the past to the England of the Middle Ages. In researching the novel, Avi referred to more than two hundred books — some about the 1381 Peasants' Revolt that forms the backdrop for the novel and others about the people and their daily lives.

Dear Avi,

A body hanging limply from the gallows, his dead body swaying in the wind . . .

I was repulsed, but intrigued. I could not put down your book *Crispin: The Cross of Lead*. It caused my heart to beat rapidly in suspense. I was so inspired by your vivid, descriptive voice in this historical novel that I want to become a writer. I want the ability to accurately describe a scene for readers so that they believe they are actually there.

A good writer, I believe, should want a reader to learn, wonder, and question. After reading your book, I became fascinated with the Middle Ages. What was that time really like? I ran to the library, scoured for books about knights, and continued reading about the subject. You opened my mind to a new area of interest. You also made me believe I was actually in the novel. I could picture the scenery. I became one of the characters. I fought with a sword and ate with the people. For a short time, I became part of the book.

I want to be a writer that opens up doors for people. I want to set scenes and describe occupations that not everyone can become. People may not have the physical or mental capabilities to be an astronaut, race-car driver, teacher, dancer, or baseball player, but for a time, I want them to experience what each of those professions would be like.

I am a ten-year-old boy. I have mild cerebral palsy, but for one cool fall afternoon, I became Crispin, living in the Middle Ages. Thank you for that gift.

Sincerely,

Thomas J. Cienki

"Stopping by Woods on a Snowy Evening"
ROBERT FROST

"Your poem is my winter."
Katja Saana Sinikka Martin

Robert Frost first said that he wrote "Stopping by Woods on a Snowy Evening" on a summer day in June, when the imagery came to him as if it were "an hallucination." He said he wrote the words quickly and without effort, as if the poem was already formed in his mind and just rising to the surface. However, a later essay revealed that the poem's genesis was not as Frost had publicly indicated. At a reading, he had confided to the writer of the essay that he wrote the poem at Christmastime, when he was struggling financially. He had little money and none to purchase gifts for his children. Returning from town without the hoped-for presents, he stopped in the woods and began to cry. The horse's bell woke him from his reverie.

Although born in San Francisco, California, Robert Frost spent most of his life as a New Englander. It was at his farm in southern Vermont that he wrote "Stopping by Woods on a Snowy Evening."

Dear Robert Frost,

I used to live in a world where every winter there was the assurance of snow. I would sit in the woods across from my house with my dog, watching the woods fill up with snow. I would watch as the snowflakes gracefully danced through the frozen sky, slowly descending upon the earth.

Everything has changed. I moved from Delaware to Georgia, from the North to the South. Now I live in a world where every year the temperature drops and the winter arrives, but there is no chance of snow. No white blanket is dropped over the landscape to cover the leaves of fall. Just the hard biting wind, the work with no reward.

Your poem "Stopping by Woods on a Snowy Evening" is all I have left to bring back that feeling of tranquility and simplicity. I had thought that that feeling could only be triggered by being surrounded by a world of white. Your poem is my winter. It's my snow in a small collection of words.

Sincerely,

Katja Saana Sinikka Martin

"I'm Nobody! Who Are You?"
EMILY DICKINSON

"It's true. Nobody wants to talk to the nobodies."
Erica Langan

"I have dared to do strange things — bold things," Emily Dickinson wrote in a letter to a former school friend in 1850. Her boldness was to lead her down a path that was unusual for young women in the mid-nineteenth century: to find personal fulfillment and creative expression through the writing of poetry. At the time, Christian reforms throughout New England had sparked a religious fever, but Dickinson did not succumb to it. Unusual, too, were her ambivalent feelings toward marriage. She did not marry and so was never bound to or dependent on a husband, as many of her friends were. She also limited her involvement in what she perceived as tiring social visits, treasuring her family and solitude. Through her letters and poems, she expressed her independence in her unique, deeply felt view of the world.

Dear Emily Dickinson,

I remember a trip to Borders bookstore with my mom. As we were walking down the aisles filled with hundreds of books, all of them calling our names, she stopped and pulled out a slim book with a creamy blue cover.

"Emily Dickinson," she murmured. "She's a really good poet. Here, look at a couple of poems." And with that, she handed me the book, neither of us aware of how powerful the treasures within truly were. I opened the book to a random page and began reading. Well, I don't know if you could call it reading, because, unfortunately, I was finding it difficult to understand a single line. "They're very deep poems," my mom told me. "A lot of them might be difficult to understand."

I was on the verge of putting the book back in its place, of leaving it in the bookstore to await another, more experienced reader, when I had a thought. *I can't just leave this book here!* I thought with defiance. Because even though I couldn't really understand whole poems, I could understand enough to recognize the beauty and the depth of your writing, and surely no one in their right mind could leave something like that behind. So I announced to my mom that I wanted to buy it.

The whole ride home, I was searching the collection of poems, reading my ever-changing favorites to my mom, who listened intently. She's a big fan of yours, too. As I read on, I began to realize something. Although maybe I couldn't comprehend a couple of words, or couldn't fully understand a line or two, I was beginning to understand many of the messages burrowed deep beneath the printed words. Eventually, I came across your poem that begins, "I'm Nobody! Who are you?"

This poem truly spoke to me, because sometimes, I do feel like nobody. Emily, you made me feel like being a nobody is so much more fun than being somebody, and you made me agree with you. Also, you made me feel like I'm not alone. The fact that someone as brilliant and as influential as you could call yourself a nobody makes me feel like everyone exciting, everyone worth anything in this world, is a nobody, and all of the somebodies are the boring, plain people who are really just trying too hard to be somebody.

I think one of the best lines in this poem is "They'd banish us, you know." That line stuck out to me, mostly because of the simplicity of it. It's true. Nobody wants to talk to the nobodies, because no one wants to *be* nobody. They want to be somebody, because, even if nobodies are far superior, somebodies are the ones who get noticed, the ones who become rich and famous. Everyone casts off the nobodies, because who ever dreams of being nobody? The answer: nobody.

Emily, your poem showed me the wonders of being a nobody, and how, even if there's not a spotlight shining down on you, the light inside of you is the brightest of all, brighter than any camera flash.

Erica Langan

Forged by Fire
Sharon Draper

"I used to find it hard to forgive my dad."
Taaja Immani Draughn

"I learned to dream through reading," says Sharon Draper, who has won numerous awards for her realistic novels of teens confronting difficult situations in their lives. Before she became a best-selling author, however, Sharon Draper was an English teacher at a high school in Cincinnati. One day in a local store, she witnessed a disturbing scene: a mother verbally threatening her three-year-old child, who was seated in a shopping cart. That night, she began to write about what she had seen and heard. After reading Draper's story, author Alex Haley wrote her an admiring letter. She never forgot those words of encouragement from a much-respected and widely published author to one who was just starting out.

Sharon Draper's books also contain unforgettable words of encouragement. In 1997 she was named National Teacher of the Year; the same year, her novel *Forged by Fire*, about a boy trying to protect his younger sister from an abusive father and a drug-addicted mother, was published.

Dear Sharon Draper,

Thank you for writing *Forged by Fire* and understanding what I'm going through. My father departed from me when I was two years old. I am hurt by his absence every day.

I never had father-to-daughter talks like my girlfriends. Some girls can call their dad in times of need. They have their fathers to give them a hug and say "Everything's going to be okay." But not me. Instead, my mama and I would have those talks. Even though my mama tries, I still feel like there's something missing. While Mama tries to comfort me, deep down I want my dad to be the one to tell me how to handle so-called friends and peer pressure.

One day my mama was talking to me about one of your books. Honestly, I didn't think I would like them, but I went to the library and checked one out — *Forged by Fire*. After reading the first two chapters, I just couldn't keep my hands off of it. I was scared for Gerald when his house was on fire and he was left there alone. I was mad at Jordan because Gerald's aunt Queen died at the hospital and all he cared about was the baseball game.

As I got deeper into the book, my dad popped into my head. When I *am* able to visit my dad, we don't have much time to spend together and very little privacy. So we don't get to finish our conversations or I can't say what I want because someone may be listening. After our visits, my dad will send me a letter reminiscing about our chat. Or he may have some questions to ask me about something I said. My dad's letters make me feel comfortable and happy. To me, his letters show that he was listening and he cares. Sometimes, he will send me "just thinking about you cards" or Bible verses he wants me to memorize.

When I finally finished your book, I understood the meaning of the expression "forgive and forget." *Forgive* means to apologize. *Forget* means to move on with your life. I used to find it hard to forgive my dad, then forget what he has done (or is unable to do). *Forged by Fire* taught me to release old pain so I won't miss out on my dad's love. Gerald and I couldn't release old pain because we were hurt so badly in the past. At last we see that there is a way to throw out our old pain and finally forgive and forget. I finally understand that love can do this.

That's why I'm going to forgive and forget that my father can't be around in my life because he's been in prison for the last nine years.

Thank you for understanding,
Taaja Immani Draughn

Out of My Mind
SHARON DRAPER

"The only person who didn't understand
anything was me."
Jayanth Uppaluri

Sharon Draper says that in working on her novel *Out of My Mind*, she kept an eye on "accuracy of fact as well as sincerity of spirit." Since the book's main character, Melody, has cerebral palsy, Draper wanted to be sure to depict the factual details of her condition accurately. Further, although Draper says that Melody is not a portrayal of her own daughter who has a disability, she adds that her experiences trying to communicate with her daughter gave her insight into Melody's perspective. Most important, Draper says, she did not want the reader to pity Melody. She wanted to capture Melody's intelligence and spunk and let the reader "see" inside her mind. She hopes the book will help her readers "get it right" in real life — truly seeing, rather than staring at or turning away from, people with disabilities.

Dear Sharon Draper,

I don't have cerebral palsy. I don't need a device to communicate. I don't even have a photographic memory. My life is so different from Melody's life. I can use all of my fingers to type on a computer. I can walk around the block. I can take part in a regular conversation about the St. Louis Cardinals. I don't need an aide to help me. I have two siblings: a brother and a sister. My sister is about as free of disabilities as you can get. My brother is a different story.

My brother has difficulty in expressing his words because he has a form of autism. Like Melody, he tries to tell people many things, and like Melody, he gets frustrated when people don't understand him. Similar to Melody, he has a device to help him communicate, but unlike Melody's, my brother's device is quite complicated to use. On top of this, he does not always have his device when he needs it the most because the battery can fail at any time.

Because of his talking complications, people don't understand him, and sadly he gets frustrated. What's so hard to understand about this? If I had trouble expressing myself, I would be frustrated, too. For example, if I couldn't tell my parents that I hated peas and they kept giving me peas, or if I couldn't tell them that I love eggnog and they kept offering me carrot juice . . . I think you get the picture. When my brother gets frustrated, he might tear paper or throw things. Sometimes, to get attention, he has even hurt himself by hitting his head or banging his chin. Before

I read your book, I never understood how he could survive or how to help him.

Then I read your book. Though cerebral palsy is different from autism, there are some things in common. People with cerebral palsy or autism are held back by symptoms, whether it's lack of mobility or lack of expression. Also people with autism are not dumb, and the same goes for people with cerebral palsy. Reading *Out of My Mind* gave me a different perspective on things. It is the only book I have read that was from the impaired person's perspective. I never thought *What is she crying about?* because I could vividly see what Melody was thinking.

Your book made me think differently about my brother and begin to put myself in his shoes. I began to help him express his feelings. For example, when I ask him a question, I give him time to respond rather than ask him over and over again like I used to. I also have learned how to interact with my brother. We wrestle together and chase each other around the house instead of doing things separately. Before I read your book, I didn't make the effort to play with him. That was a big mistake, because seeing my brother's winning smile when we played for the first time has made me realize that we have a very special bond that no one can break.

It is important for Melody to feel confident in order to succeed, and that's very important for my brother, too, just as it is for any of us. When Melody participates in the Whiz Kids competition, her family and her caregiver,

Mrs. V, support her and help her study, which gives her the confidence to win. It is also vital for my brother to experience success. When my mom wants him to watch videos and he brings her the iPad, we don't overlook it. We praise him for doing it. This gives him the confidence to do better and progress. If he hides in the closet and stuffs his face with Lindt chocolate truffles without asking, we don't scream at him. Instead, we take the bag away, tell him to ask us first . . . then we all stuff our faces with chocolate. Instead of making him afraid of us, this makes him laugh, and it makes us happy because we get to eat chocolate (chocolate equals treasure in our house). When he flashes his million-dollar smile at us as we are eating chocolate, it sends an unspoken message that words could never express.

Now I know that my brother *can* survive. When Melody is in Mr. Dimming's class and everyone thinks it's a mistake that she got 100% on the preliminary Whiz Kids test, she doesn't give up. She studies very hard with Mrs. V and then aces the final test to get into the Whiz Kids competition. This made me think that my brother can survive all that he is going through and that people around him will realize how intelligent he is. If Melody could endure all the taunts and insults given by Molly and Claire, my brother can endure the ignorant people who don't understand him. If Melody can tolerate not making it to the national Whiz Kids competition, my brother can tolerate his challenges. He works so hard in his therapies, and I am confident it will pay off.

Before I read your book, I thought my brother didn't understand me. Because he couldn't talk that well, I didn't think he could understand anyone. After I read your book, I realized something. I was wrong. He understands me. The only person who didn't understand anything was me. Thanks for writing this amazing book that helped me to understand my brother.

Jayanth Uppaluri

The Diary of a Young Girl
ANNE FRANK

"I can hide from being Jewish. You couldn't."
Eliana Kahn

"When I write I can shake off all my cares," Anne Frank wrote in her diary. The little autograph book with its red-and-white plaid cover was a gift from her parents on her thirteenth birthday. But just a few weeks later, the spread of Nazism into Holland, where the Franks lived, endangered the nation's Jews. Leaving the country was not possible, so Anne's father arranged a hiding place for the family, a secret apartment shared with another family on the top floors behind a business Otto Frank had owned. Lonely, Anne imagined a friend named Kitty — and filled the pages of the autograph book with letters to her.

After months in hiding and learning of the death of so many Jewish people, Anne let her despair overflow onto the pages. She wrote, "I've reached the point where I hardly care whether I live or die. The world will keep on turning without me, and I can't do anything to change events anyway." A few weeks later, however, she rose above her sorrow, stating that despite the horrors of war, she still believed people were good at heart.

By the time her family was found out, arrested, and sent to concentration camps, Anne had written hundreds of pages about her life while hiding in "the Secret Annex."

Dear Anne Frank,

I struggle a lot with being Jewish. Every year around Christmastime, I feel like the only one who's not talking about Santa and Christmas trees. There are Santas around every corner saying "Merry Christmas," and through the windows of houses I can see big tall trees with glittering ornaments and happy presents just sitting there waiting to be opened. Every magazine I open says "Get your Christmas presents here." Even the job listings say things like "Have the chimney cleaned so Santa will have a clean landing!" I feel like I am surrounded by people who don't know what the word *Hanukkah* means. When I was younger, I felt jealous. Now that I am older, I realize that I just feel lonely.

I could always join the crowd. It's not that hard to pretend. All you do is, when kids talk about Christmas, smile and laugh and talk about what is on your wish list. I get really tempted to do this. But then I think about you. My grandfather gave me your book last year. At first I did not want to read it. I was tired of having to think about being Jewish. It was part of me that others did not really want to look at and see. My parents told me that *The Diary of a Young Girl* was a really important book, so I doubtfully started to read it.

At first, your book seemed to be about normal teenage-girl thoughts. Then it turned upside down. Your story — well, your life — got really gray and dark and scary. Jews weren't allowed to go to stores or movies. Soon you couldn't even go to school. Then you weren't allowed outside. Your diary changed, and it seemed as if it was written by a completely different person. I think that it *was* written by a completely different person — someone who was allowed only to be Jewish. I can hide from being Jewish. You couldn't. You were really proud of being Jewish.

You would have rather died as a Jew than lived behind a mask. You gave up so much. It makes me want to carry on your name as a young Jewish girl. I'm studying for my bat mitzvah, and whenever I study the Torah, I always think about you and how you never got to have one. On the day of my bat mitzvah, I hope you will be there, standing right next to me, reciting and praying along with me.

Eliana Kahn

Shades of Black
Sandra L. Pinkney

"In my opinion, diversity is a good thing."
Chelsea Brown

"To my vanilla, my butter pecan, and my chocolate," reads the dedication of Sandra Pinkney's picture book *Shades of Black*. The book, illustrated with photographs by her husband, Myles, celebrates the diversity of black children and culture. Comparing skin color to popcorn and pretzels, ice cream and peaches, Pinkney inspires children just learning how to read to appreciate their uniqueness. But as Chelsea explains below in her letter to Sandra, learning how to view oneself — and to like what you see — is a challenge that older children face as well.

Dear Sandra L. Pinkney,
    The first time I opened your book *Shades of Black* was about six years ago. But not once in those six years did I really take the time to think about the book's message. I was young and didn't understand the book's true meaning until several years later, and it never even crossed my

mind that this book would become a great help at my new school.

In 2011, my family moved from Massachusetts to Mechanicsville, Virginia. Everything at my new school was normal. I had a teacher who occasionally yelled and sometimes gave hugs. I was feeling great until the middle of the year, when we started learning about the Civil War. This was the first time we were learning about slavery in school. I was one out of three brown-skinned kids in my class, and when my teacher said, "Black people were owned and traded as slaves," everyone else turned to look at us. I was very embarrassed and, at that moment, I wished I did not have brown skin. I wanted to be the same complexion as most of the other students. Brown was the color of dirt and mud; I thought it was bad to be black.

One night I was sitting in my room mourning over the incident in class. When I'm sad, I normally read, so I grabbed the book *Shades of Black* from my bookshelf. I read the first page: "I am black. I am unique." For the first time, I really thought about this sentence. It was true that I was one of a few African Americans at my school. So, technically that made me unique. I felt a little better, but not a hundred percent. I continued to the second page: "I am the creamy white frost in vanilla ice cream." I was surprised because I thought that no black people could have such light skin. I continued: "I am . . . the gingery brown in a cookie." I said, "Hey, that's my color skin." I knew people had my type of skin, but the girl on the page looked just like me. I felt really good after finishing the book.

Sometimes it makes you think that just because someone has different color skin, speaks a different language, or is from a different country, that doesn't mean that they are better or worse than someone else. We all come in different sizes, shapes, and colors. We have different backgrounds and different experiences. In my opinion, diversity is a good thing.

I am now nine years old, and I ignore the stares when the words "African American" or "slave" come up during school. We still learn about things like slavery, but do I get embarrassed or feel bad about myself? Not at all. "I am black. I am unique." I am proud to be me.

Chelsea Brown

The Yearling
Marjorie Kinnan Rawlings

"When it seems like I'm all alone, I'm really not."
Lacie Craven Glidden

Restless and unsatisfied as an urban journalist, Marjorie Kinnan Rawlings purchased a seventy-two-acre farm in the Florida scrub country with her husband. She described their land near Cross Creek as "primitive" and "off the beaten path," with "mysterious swamps" and "great live oaks, dripping gray Spanish moss." She raised ducks, grew vegetables, fished for crabs and turtles, hunted alligator, and wrote.

Her book *The Yearling* was published in 1938; it's about a young boy in the Florida wilderness who rescues and befriends a fawn he names Flag. It won the Pulitzer Prize for fiction and brought Rawlings fame. She had retreated into the wilderness, away from what she called "urban confusion," and in doing so, had found her writer's voice and her subjects.

Dear Mrs. Rawlings,

I live near the ocean, under a mountain, on a farm. We raise a lot of different animals, but mostly sheep. We also hunt for our food. These things made me feel very close to the characters in *The Yearling*. If you have sheep, you have orphaned lambs. If you have orphaned lambs, you have true friends. They get into a lot of trouble (a lot like Flag!) but it's all worth it to have a little lamb that follows you and is dependent on you.

I remember Mattie, a lamb whose mother had refused to take her. I heated up her bottle and fed her every two to three hours every day of her life. She would kick up her heels and run with me down the road, then push her plush little head into my hand. We would lie in the grass, and I talked with her about everything, and she listened as I felt her fragile little hoof and followed her tiny, warm curls. One day she got sick. I kept watch over her the whole day, praying hard and making her as comfortable as possible. I picked her up and held her tight, tracing the little swirl on the side of her face. I hoped to feel her lean her head against me. She didn't. She was dead. I reluctantly put her down and looked at her for the last time, then covered her with a towel, stepped back, and said good-bye through tears to my lifeless friend. Afterward, I ran to the barn in secret and cried into my sister's lamb until it was time to feed him.

After each death, it feels like you lost a child. It is so devastating. I cry and feel like I did something wrong, like

I could have prevented their deaths. I felt like I had trusted in God and He let me down, like He had forgotten about me. Why did He give me something only to take it away? Why didn't He heal her when I asked?

The answer came in your book. When I read about Jody and his fawn, at first I asked the same question. Why does this happen? Then I saw what Flag taught him. All my lambs had been working unintentionally to help me become who I am today, and who I will be. They taught me how to deal with challenges in my life, how to overcome them. When it seems like I'm all alone, I'm really not.

If I could change the past and bring Mattie back to life, I wouldn't. I look back now and I only smile. I continue to raise sheep, and always happiness prevails over death. When it seems like there is no good left in the world, you see it displayed in indirect ways. For every sad thing, there's a happy reason behind it, and it makes us stronger people. We can find rest in this. Thank you for writing this book.

Lacie Craven Glidden

Dog Years
MARK DOTY

"Mushy answers don't feel true."
Darius Atefat-Peckham

"Not only was I the new kid, but I wore glasses, had a Southern accent, and was chubby," Mark Doty says about switching schools often as a child. His closest friends became those he met within books. "This was especially true with books about animals," he says. In 2008, Mark Doty's book of poems *Fire to Fire* won the National Book Award for poetry. He has also written nonfiction, including the memoir *Dog Years*, about Beau and Arden, the golden and black retrievers Doty adopted from shelters and who became his "secret heroes."

Dear Mark Doty,

I'm a sucker for dogs. Specifically for golden retrievers. Specifically for golden retrievers on the cover of books — like yours, *Dog Years*. While shopping with my dad for books one day, I passed by a table with *Dog Years* displayed in the middle. Unfortunately, I had forgotten my wallet (my dad's frequent complaint) and had to beg him to buy me your book.

"Please, Dad," I said, "it's by . . . Mark Doty." Honestly, I didn't know who you were then. I just loved the picture on the front because it looks like the dog—your dog, Beau, I'd discover—is pleading with shoppers to buy the book, with his big brown eyes and perked-up ears. But it would take more than begging to convince Dad this time. I knew he'd remind me that I had five books at home I hadn't read yet. (I'm a sucker for books, too.)

"Mark Doty, the poet?" Dad asked, grabbing the book from my hands.

All it took, apparently, was your name.

You see, my dad is a poet, too, and so was my mom, before she died in a car accident eight years ago this February. My six-year-old brother also died in the accident, leaving me and my dad to face a world without them. I was only three at the time and didn't understand what was happening. When I asked, everyone told me Mama and Cyrus went on a long journey and I wouldn't see them for a while. It was a difficult time for my dad and me. I missed the attention I usually got from my older brother, so at meetings with my dad's boarding school students, I often tried to steal the boys' attention, dancing and breaking things accidentally around them.

One night Dad surprised me. He knew of a litter of golden retrievers that the school's theater director was selling. Dad told me that he'd thought about it, and I could have one. Sure enough, one week later, fuzzy and chubby Jack-Jack entered our family. He quickly ate Dad's favorite Tony Lama cowboy boots, he left "presents" on the kitchen floor, and he rolled in dead squirrels and rotting birds behind our apartment. So I giggled when your Beau smothers himself in cow poop, and your other dog, Arden, rolls in whale blubber that looks to you like a mattress that's washed up on shore. What is it about smelling horrendous that thrills dogs? you ask. My thoughts exactly.

You raise other questions that are harder to answer. What is death, anyway? What do living things feel in those final moments? And most of all, what do we do with all this sadness, every time someone we love dies? Most people wouldn't consider this a book kids could understand, or should read. But I wish that adults understood that mushy answers don't feel true, and they don't comfort us. Sometimes they make me feel even sadder.

Now Jack-Jack is almost seven (and still fuzzy and chubby), and I can't begin to tell you what he means to me. Maybe I don't have to — I think you already know. As you explain in *Dog Years*, Beau came into your life just as your partner, Wally, was dying. For both of you, Beau was a golden ray of light, a very special animal who teaches you a lot about life and death, and who helps you through it. You remind us that dogs have their own feelings. They have spirits just as big as ours. Even though they don't have the power of speech, that doesn't mean they aren't capable of "speaking" directly to our hearts. As you write, "Maybe we should be glad, finally, that the word can't go where the heart can, not completely." It's freeing, to think there's always an aspect of us outside the grasp of speech, the common stuff of language. Maybe that's why I am never more comforted than when Jack-Jack is by my side, licking the tears from my cheeks when I fall or just feel sad. I don't have to explain. I can just be with him, and he wags his tail, or licks my hand, or just looks at me with that tiny glint in his eye — some spark of thought. Of love.

Books have been my great friends, too. I take yours with me to bed every night to read with my new mom, Rachie. Jack-Jack is always by the floor, listening to your words about Wally, Beau, and Arden. Sometimes Rachie and I lie beside him on the floor (despite his breath), petting him as we read. Who would've thought that just a single book could bond us like that and remind us of what we have, even as we've lost so much?

That day in the bookstore, I was just looking for a good story about a dog like mine. The only one who sings along whenever I practice the recorder. The one who always greets me at the door with a playful growl. I don't know what I'll do the day when he won't be there waiting. But I know I'll have your book to guide me through it. In many ways, it already has, and I thank you.

Darius Atefat-Peckham

The Running Dream
Wendelin Van Draanen

"Life is a big stinking blob of mess."
Gerel Sanzhikov

"I'm an adult," says author Wendelin Van Draanen, but "on the inside I'm stuck at thirteen." For ten years she wrote books, sending her manuscripts to publishers and receiving rejection letters. Reading *Dandelion Wine* by Ray Bradbury triggered an idea — not about *what* to write but about *how* to write it: from the perspective and in the voice of a thirteen-year-old. "That's when things clicked for me," she says.

As someone who is stuck at thirteen, she truly likes kids that age, but she also remembers that middle school was torture. And that feeds her stories. "As a writer, you are supposed to put your main character in uncomfortable situations," she says. And she does: in *The Running Dream*, Jessica has lost a leg in a car accident. To make matters worse, Jessica is a runner.

Dear Wendelin Van Draanen,

I have never lost a leg. I was not born with cerebral palsy. I do not use a wheelchair. I do not have speech problems. But I have lost the one thing I loved the most. My family is made up of my dad, my two grandmothers, my sister, and me. Where is my mom? Look above you. She has landed among the stars.

My mom battled cancer for two years. We lost her in September of 2012. I remember when my mom was first diagnosed; she started losing her hair a couple strands at a time. Next thing you know, she was almost bald. Your character Jessica and my mom both lost something important. Out of nowhere, Jessica lost her leg in a car accident. My mom lost most of her hair. They both lost some of their pride. Life is funny, you know? Like at first, your life is going perfect and you have everything you could wish for, and just like that . . . it's gone. Everything is ripped apart. Simply just . . . gone.

I was heartbroken. My mom looked miserable. I could not stand seeing her suffer like that. She needed countless doses of medicine and weekly chemotherapy. She went through the same cycle for two years. But on a beautiful sunny afternoon, she grew wings. She was an angel in heaven and she was flying in the sky. I was downcast, but also happy that she was free from suffering. Before I read your book, I never thought I could be joyful again.

But then I read it. I have realized that I am not the only one who has this problem. As I was reading *The Running*

Dream, I saw how difficult it was for Jessica to adjust to such a dramatic change and I could relate. Jessica needed to use a prosthetic leg and learn how to walk with crutches. I needed to embrace the fact that my mom was in a better place. Reading your book gave me a different perspective on things. I thought I would never be happy again, but when I read how Jessica got her running leg and practiced running little by little, I realized that I could jump back on track, too. When her teacher showed her the YouTube video of the running amputee, she thought, *Maybe I can run again*. And so did I.

I could not put your book down as I was reading. One of the reasons I fell in love with it is that it is so inspiring. You would never think that a girl like Jessica — popular, pretty, and perfect — would become friends with a girl like Rosa — who has cerebral palsy and uses a wheelchair. I love how your novel shows that anything is possible if you believe and try. Jessica and Rosa develop a bond that will never break.

Your book moved me in a way that no book has ever done before — it gave me hope. By reading *The Running Dream*, I have learned many things. I have always wondered why I was never happy, besides the fact that my mom had passed. But then it hit me. If I spent the rest of my life focusing on all the negative elements, I would never be able to enjoy all the little things that make up a good life.

Your book also taught me that when life knocks you down, you just need to pick yourself up and keep on moving. When Jessica lost her leg, it did not stop her from pursuing her dream. And I am not going to spend the rest of my life feeling sorry for myself. I will live life to the fullest and live like there is no tomorrow.

During the two years that my mom has not been here, I have realized that only one thing has kept my life together, and that is hope. So thank you. Thank you for giving me that. I know that the life I live is not perfection, but it is enough for now. One of the most important things I have learned is that life is a big stinking blob of mess, but that's the glory of it, too.

Gerel Sanzhikov

"Hug o' War"
SHEL SILVERSTEIN

"Maybe your words weren't meant just for me."
Anna Mytko

An editor at Simon and Schuster told Shel Silverstein it would never sell. The fifty-page manuscript he had written was a fable about a relationship between a child and a generous tree. The editor thought the book fell between the cracks — not for children and yet not quite right for adults, either. The editor was wrong. Picked up by Ursula Nordstrom, an editor whose goal was to publish "good books for bad children," *The Giving Tree* became a bestseller and a classic of children's literature, as did Silverstein's volumes of poetry. Filled with sometimes zany creatures like the Bloath and with radical ideas like replacing tug-of-war with hug-of-war, Silverstein's books encourage children to act out, push the limits, and explore the world.

Dear Shel Silverstein,

I was five years old and had one end of a jump rope in my mouth and my twin brother had the other in his mouth. It was a fierce game of tug-of-war and neither of us was going to give up. Competing against my brother was natural for me and serious business. We played for about ten minutes before getting tired. Just as I was going to win by forcing my brother to my side of the room, he gave one particularly hard game-ending tug. I saw blood, realized that my first tooth had been jerked out, and started bawling. Then I stopped. I actually had beaten my twin at something. I was the first to lose a tooth!

At seven years old, I came upon what would become my favorite poem of yours, called "Hug o' War," and was instantly reminded of how I painfully lost my first tooth. I took the poem literally. Your words seemed to be a warning not to play tug-of-war, but to try and hug instead. I felt as if you knew me and that this poem was written with me in mind. I loved this feeling of connection to a famous person and felt important.

When I was nine, I chose "Hug o' War" to recite in school. The class loved this clever poem, and I remember thinking that maybe your words weren't meant just for me. Maybe the warning was more of a suggestion and was actually for all kids in my class and school. We should all be kinder to each other, hug and play, and we would all "win." I loved the feeling of having found a poem that made me feel connected to my classmates. They smiled as I read and I felt important.

Reading "Hug o' War" now, at age eleven, I realize that my first interpretations were correct, but also not quite right. I can see that "Hug o' War" is a gentle, playful suggestion for the entire world. If everyone was nice, the world would be a better place and society would run better. When you say "and everyone hugs instead of tugs" you mean that cooperating instead of fighting would make all of humanity "win." Since I figured out this bigger way of thinking about "Hug o' War," I like this poem even more. I love this feeling of better understanding a poem and feel it is important that the world read "Hug o' War."

My family loves your poems, Mr. Silverstein. We can read them over the course of our lives and keep learning from them. Thank you for sharing your amazing talent with the world. Without poetry like yours, people would have no way to hear literature in a different way. Maybe a short, clever poem can help them understand the concepts of life more easily. Had I hugged and not tugged my brother that day, we would have both won the game. If everyone could hug, giggle, wiggle, kiss, cuddle, and grin, then the world would truly be a better place.

Best wishes,
Anna Mytko

Eva of the Farm
DIA CALHOUN

"The spiraling piece of lead had shattered my heart."
Linnea Rain Lentfer

"Nature brings us fully alive," writes Dia Calhoun. She also says that she didn't completely understand the power of nature to restore the human spirit until she began writing *Eva of the Farm*. As a young girl, Calhoun first fell in love with reading and writing during visits to the school library. But years later, it was her father-in-law's apple orchard in eastern Washington that inspired her to write about Eva. In the novel, blight has damaged the trees on Eva's family's farm, and the farm is in danger of foreclosure. The fear of losing her home spurs Eva, who writes poetry, into action to try to save what she loves best.

Dear Dia Calhoun,

In my first ten years of life I had always considered a loss a loss. I could find nothing good out of it. A fear was something I would avoid, not face.

I come from a family of hunters. Each year we go to a small cabin on an island and spend the days walking slowly through the beauty of the southeast Alaskan old-growth forest. From this, we not only take in beauty, but we also take the lives of what I believe to be the most graceful and peaceful of animals on earth: the Sitka black-tailed deer.

Every time I've heard a rifle go off and watched a deer fall, it has always seemed that the spiraling piece of lead had shattered my heart, not the deer's. As we've knelt alongside the still-warm animal, my tears left wet marks on the dark, velvety fur.

Through all the years of hunting, I've struggled to make peace in my mind between the beauty of the hunt and taking the deer's life. Reading your book *Eva of the Farm* was a big step.

As I read, I found Eva's love for her farm and her friend like my love for the woods and the deer. Her sense of loss for her friend and possibly her home was like mine. I was able to relate so well with Eva in the beginning that as she made peace with her troubles, so did I.

Now, as I walk up to a deer, the tears falling are not of sorrow; they are of gratitude, to be able to live where I do and experience the bittersweet beauty of hunting.

Linnea Rain Lentfer

Hoot
CARL HIAASEN

"I have not done anything dangerous or illegal."
Davis Klimek

Carl Hiaasen grew up on the fringe of Florida's Everglades, where he and his friends "spent many hours in the swamp catching snakes, lizards, and other critters that we brought home and hid in our basement." (The wildlife eventually escaped to terrorize the other family members.) Over time, he watched as many of the local places he loved were destroyed for the purpose of commercial and residential development. But, as a kid, he felt helpless to do anything to stop the loss of wilderness and wetlands. And his parents told him that he could not stop progress.

When an editor suggested that, after decades of investigative reporting and writing adult fiction about tough social issues, Hiaasen might write a children's book about environmental themes, he was hesitant. But his childhood provided all the incentive he needed to start writing *Hoot*. And in his children's books, his characters can and do call a halt to development and successfully fight for the protection of wilderness and wetlands.

Dear Mr. Hiaasen,

Two years ago, I read your book *Hoot*. Mother Paula's Pancake House being built on the site of endangered burrowing owls and the kids' actions in the book to prevent it made me realize two important things: One, the cost of development to wildlife and wildlife habitats can be devastating and irreversible. Two, even kids can make a difference when they stand for what they believe in.

For several years, I have been going with my family and grandparents to Sea Island, Georgia, for vacation. One of the best parts of Sea Island for me is going to the beach and seeing the wildlife. Sea Island is an important nesting site for endangered loggerhead sea turtles, an animal that I love. The loggerhead sea turtles return year after year to the same nesting spot. Recently, Sea Island had a big expansion, and a new pool, movie theater, several other buildings, and condominiums were added. Most people see these developments as a good thing, but I know that the expansion has hurt the wildlife and destroyed helpless animals' homes. There is now less shoreline for the loggerhead sea turtles to nest on, and more noise and brighter lights on the beach, which will scare the sea turtles from coming on shore to nest. Like the kids in *Hoot*, who would rather see burrowing owls than a pancake house, I would rather see endangered loggerhead turtles than a movie theater.

I have not done anything dangerous or illegal to stop the development, but like the kids in *Hoot*, I am trying to make a difference. I have become friends with the Sea

Island naturalist, and I go on all of the late-night and early-morning turtle patrol walks that I can. During turtle patrols, we use special red lights and search for new sea turtle nests, which we mark with identification stakes. One morning I saw a baby loggerhead turtle hatch and make its way to the ocean — it was an incredible experience! I have also helped pass out flyers that encourage beach property owners to shut off their outdoor lights at night. This way the female turtles won't be scared to come on the beach and newly hatched baby turtles won't be confused and head away from, instead of toward, the ocean. I have also become a member of the Sea Turtle Center, which rescues sea turtles and nurses them back to health.

Mr. Hiaasen, you have opened my mind about what can happen to wildlife when there is development. People are not thinking about what they are doing to the environment when they build new buildings or destroy shorelines. *Hoot* inspired me to act, and I now know that it doesn't matter if you are big or small. If you stand up for what you believe in, you can make something happen.

Davis Klimek

One Fish, Two Fish, Red Fish, Blue Fish
DR. SEUSS

"The Keep pile, the Throw Out pile,
and the Keep in the Attic pile"
Becky Miller

"I think I had something to do with kicking Dick and Jane out of the school system," Theodor Geisel — better known as Dr. Seuss — said in 1986. "And without talking about teaching, I think I have helped kids laugh in schools as well as at home."

Dick and Jane were pleasant white children who lived in a pleasant house with Mother and Father and their baby sister, Sally. They had pleasant pets, as well — Puff the cat and Spot the dog. And they did pleasant things like playing with their dog. See Spot run. Throughout the first half of the twentieth century, the Dick and Jane primers were the tools for teaching millions of schoolchildren how to read.

Then along came Dr. Seuss. As the story goes, for Seuss's fourth children's book, the director of the education division at Houghton Mifflin gave him a list of vocabulary words for first- and second-grade students and challenged him to write a book using only those words that would interest kids. The author created *The Cat in the Hat*. The cat not only looked different from Dick and Jane's Puff, but his behavior was zany and chaotic. And unlike the dull prose of the Dick and Jane books, Dr. Seuss wrote in rhyming verse. The book was an immediate success. It was soon followed by *Green Eggs and Ham; One Fish, Two Fish, Red Fish, Blue Fish;* and many more. Learning to read in America would never be the same.

Dear Dr. Seuss,

I remember reading *One Fish, Two Fish, Red Fish, Blue Fish* when I was little, at night before I went to bed, and being so absorbed in it that I wouldn't put it down. It would leave me with such a great feeling that I wouldn't want to stop reading; it was my favorite. Eventually, though, my mom would come in and tell me to go to sleep, and I always dreaded that point. I felt as if that visit was the moment my room came back to life, and I bounced back to reality. But sadly, I don't get those visits anymore. About a month ago, my mother passed away with brain cancer.

My mom always had a love of reading. She would read a two-hundred-page novel in two hours if you let her. She could read on and on and on. Most of the books she read were trashy novels, with no definite purpose except to entertain. But my mom would read me any book in the universe if I asked her to, simply because she wanted to share her love of reading with everyone. We read *One Fish, Two Fish* so many times, I can't imagine how she didn't feel as if she had written it herself, but the funny pictures, the made-up words, the voice — it made us both escape into a place we couldn't explain. It was wonderful and so exciting, it left me with a lasting impression of books I'll never forget. These memories are some I will always cherish. They connect me to my mom, and I hope one day, if I have a family, I will share these memories with my kids and pass them on. I hope I will be just like my mother, because these memories were some I shared with her.

Once, when I was about eight years old, my mom and I cleaned out my bookshelf. It was overflowing with picture books, books I had gotten as presents, and the books my mom had saved since she was a little girl. We took every single book out and made three piles: the Keep pile, the Throw Out pile, and the Keep in the Attic pile. I would take the books that no one read anymore, put them in the Throw Out pile, and as soon as my mom saw what I had done, she'd say, "NO! We have to keep this one. Don't you remember reading this?" I'd say, "Mom, I'm never going to read that again. If you really want to keep it, put it in the Attic pile." Pretty soon the Attic pile was by far the biggest one. We stored them up there, but they were soon long forgotten, isolated from small children's hands and eagerness to read for so long. I still have those Attic books, and I haven't looked at them in forever. My mother cared way too much about the memories of reading books with my brother and me when we were kids to throw them away. She and I wanted to hold on to the happy past and the fun memories. I realized that I would be okay as long as I didn't let go of our time together, just like neither of us let go of our memories reading *One Fish, Two Fish*.

One of the only books in the Keep pile was *One Fish, Two Fish*. It was the memory that always made neither of us want to let it go. Whenever I miss my mom, I can read it and remember the way her voice sounded and how safe and warm we felt with each other and the way she'd fall asleep on my bed sometimes if we read late enough. Even if I can't be with her, I can still turn to what we both held on to. I'll always have that.

"Today is gone. Today was fun. Tomorrow is another one." — Dr. Seuss
Becky Miller

The Lions of Little Rock
KRISTIN LEVINE

"In the future it will be my turn to carry on what my grandparents and parents have fought for."
Aleema Kelly

"Even as a child, I was very interested in issues of moral fairness and doing what was right," says Kristin Levine. "My parents have always been interested in social justice as well, and I guess that rubbed off on me." Levine's novel *The Lions of Little Rock* is set in 1958 in Little Rock, Arkansas, one year after the integration of Central High School. Based solidly on historical fact, the book focuses on the fictional friendship of two girls who challenge the racism of the times. Levine, who calls herself an optimist, believes that anyone who cares about equality and social justice can be a voice for change.

Dear Kristin Levine,

Your book *Lions of Little Rock* inspired me in many ways. I literally couldn't put it down, even though my parents told me I needed to go to sleep. I went into school exhausted the next day and told my library teacher all of

the things I learned from your book. In part of the conversation, he told me that my grandma had fought for civil
rights during the time period in your book.

I am black. I am white. I am both. My grandpa was a
black man. He was a member of the Black Panthers. My
grandma is white and Jewish and was educated in a college
in the North. She fought and marched in the civil rights
movement. She participated in picketing, sit-ins, protests,
and marches. She got married to a black man at a time
when the Jim Crows laws in twenty-three states made it
illegal for a white to marry a black, but she did it anyway,
even when her parents disapproved. She marched in 1963
in the March on Washington with Martin Luther King Jr.
She sacrificed her family and friends to fight for the rights
of others. I wondered why my grandma kept fighting for
the rights of black people when she was teased or when
people like her parents were not happy with her decision
and told her not to do what she did. I think my grandma
was really courageous because she chose the fight for equality over her family.

After I finished your book, I looked up my grandma
online. I couldn't believe how many videos I saw of her.
Some were interviews of her speaking for equal rights for
blacks; some were at events like funerals for other black
civil rights leaders. There was even a book that she wrote
some chapters in. I then thought of the idea of making
questions to ask my grandma. My first question was: Were

you treated differently when people found out that you were fighting for the rights of blacks?

Your book helped me understand more about history and inspired me to learn more about my family, my grandmother, my grandfather, and the rest of my family. I know now that my grandmother's experience and choices made my father who he is, and his choices for me make me who I am today. My parents can afford to send me to a private school, but they chose to send me to an integrated inner-city magnet school and I am glad they did. In the future it will be my turn to carry on what my grandparents and parents have fought for and stood for, to help the United States of America be the best it can be!

Aleema Kelly

Stargirl

Jerry Spinelli

"Even in a sea of clovers, flowers find each other."
Hillary V. Schiff

Author Jerry Spinelli believes most kids who conform to peer pressure don't really want to follow the herd and please the crowd. They just don't know how not to. "Peer pressure is just that: pressure," he says. "*Stargirl*, I guess, provides a relief valve for that pressure. Permission to be different. Permission to be oneself."

Since its publication in 2000, *Stargirl* has sold more than one million copies. The author, who has written more than thirty books, says his "library" of ideas is composed of his memories of growing up, as well as his experience helping his six children — and now his twenty-one grandchildren — grow up. He insists he doesn't write stories for children. Instead, he writes about them and all the weird and wonderful and frightening things that happen to kids while they are just being kids.

Dear Mr. Jerry Spinelli,

Sometimes in a vast meadow, full of small insignificant clovers, there is a flower. Not just any flower; this flower is special and shines more brightly and vibrantly than the others. She is beautiful. She beams at the sun. Her roots dig deeper into the soil than the others. She is closer to what we stand for, what we're made of. This flower is Stargirl Caraway.

At first the clovers show nothing but admiration for this strange yet beautiful flower. They copy her, attempt to forge petals like hers for themselves. But then doubt ensnares their simple minds. They turn against her for all her differences, all her love, all her uniqueness and compassion. They leave her. But a true stargirl is never alone. The flower knows that one day another will enter her life. She looks out beyond the setting sun.

I like to think of myself as a flower, too. The book *Stargirl* helped make me one. I wear what I like to wear, dance if I want to dance. I always stay true to myself no matter what others think. I leave pennies wherever I go in hope that one day one will bring joy to whoever finds it. Stargirl Caraway touched my heart, and I will never be the same again.

Stargirl also helped me realize that I am never alone. I have my family. And friends will always come in time. Stargirl gave me the courage to brave school without any former friends, hoping to meet new "flowers." Without her,

I would never have discovered my now most treasured friendships.

The flower petals touch, her yellow ones against his blue. They look out at the sky together. The moon is so luminous, the stars so close. Both are smiling. Even in a sea of clovers, flowers find each other. Bloom on, Stargirl!

Sincerely,

Hillary V. Schiff

A New Awareness

"Some of the pages were falling out, so I set the book gingerly on my desk. The book was old, and I wondered if it were best left on the shelf. I nearly did put *Lord of the Flies* back on the shelf, but reading it was one of the best choices I have ever made."

—Kara S. Moritz, in a letter to William Golding about his book *Lord of the Flies*

Over Sea, Under Stone
Susan Cooper

> "I left my world behind and entered a new one."
> Janet Lynne Snow

As a child in England during World War II, Susan Cooper spent many frightening nights in the family air-raid shelter. While bombs exploded outside, Susan's mother read to her children by candlelight. "Since every air raid was a reminder that an enemy was trying to kill us, I developed a very strong sense of us and them, good and evil, the Light and the Dark," Cooper remembers.

Those themes of light and darkness are the foundation of Cooper's fantasy novels. Before she became a novelist, she attended Oxford University and worked as a journalist. She soon began experimenting with fiction and discovered that the keen observation skills required of a nonfiction writer were equally important for a novelist. Decades before British author J. K. Rowling created the fantastic world of Hogwarts, Susan Cooper wrote her Dark Is Rising series, a saga about good versus evil and the power of children to save the world. The book Janet Snow writes about here is the first installment in that series.

Dear Susan Cooper,

My parents thought that I was in my room reading. They were wrong. I was inside your book. By reading the words on the page, I lived them. I never realized how your book *Over Sea, Under Stone* had changed my life until recently. I read the book a few years ago, and it changed me from someone who didn't care about reading to someone who can't put a book down.

I had read a bit before I discovered your book, but as soon as I read the first few lines, I left my world behind and entered a new one. I could see the sun-baked village of Tressiwick, and the stench of the fish at the harbor made my nose wrinkle. I shared the fear that the characters had when they were in danger. It was thrilling, more exciting than anything that I had ever read before. I loved the excitement and suspense the story created. When Barney reached up and grabbed the grail, my heart leaped, and I felt the triumph even though I had only been reading. Even now, I can still see parts of the book in my head, and I don't think that I will ever forget them.

When I finished the last word of the last line on the last page, I couldn't believe that the story was already over. The story that I had been living was still playing through my mind like a movie. I was in awe of the book. I'd never read anything like it. I'd never read something that I was pulled into, and I had never read a book that had been written on a subject that I enjoyed so much. I refused to quit talking about the book. I expounded about standing stones, the tides, and holy grails until my friends were quite fed up. But it didn't dampen the sheer pleasure I got from the book. After that, I began to read anything that looked interesting to me. I learned interesting facts from every book I read, and I got ideas that could be useful in almost any situation. My grades went up, and I was never bored when I could read. I learned that you can find anything in a book. Books made my life a great deal better, and I can trace my love of reading back to your book. When we learned about the tides in science, I immediately thought of the exceptionally low tide that your characters encountered when they went to find the cave where the grail was.

After I read your book, I began to think about life in a different way. I took more notice of things that were interesting, and I asked questions about anything I was curious about. I began to think deeply about the way time works in your book, and I finally came to my conclusion a few months ago at a Greek restaurant: I decided that time was the ultimate mystery. But the most life-changing aspect of the book was the magic that was in the words, words that pulled me into a different life. Most people say that magic is fictional, but for me it isn't. To me, magic is very real. It is the times in life where you feel like the universe is perfect, no matter what is really happening. I would never have felt magic if it hadn't been for your book.

Janet Lynne Snow

The Harry Potter book series
J. K. ROWLING

"I found myself raising my butterbeer mug
to that brave Boy Who Lived."
Anne Overton

In a Harvard University graduation speech, J. K. Rowling said, "What I feared most for myself at your age was not poverty, but failure." But failure, she said, taught her more about herself than the degree she acquired in college. She learned she had an inner strength and the discipline to pull herself out of poverty. Failure also taught her the value of her friendships. And friendship is, of course, the foundation on which Harry Potter's story unfolds.

J. K. Rowling began Harry's story in 1990, following a plan she had outlined for a seven-book series. The death of her mother, a move from England to Portugal, and a failed marriage ensued. When she returned to England with her young daughter in 1993, she had written only three chapters. She was suffering from depression. She underwent therapy, pushed forward, and just kept writing. She has called this period in her life "grim" and marked by "grinding poverty." She finished *Harry Potter and the Sorcerer's Stone* in 1995, then signed up for a teacher training course. She could not count on the book selling.

Before Harry Potter, she worked for a time as a bilingual researcher with the human rights organization Amnesty International, where she learned about "the evils humankind will inflict on their fellow humans, to gain or maintain power. But it was also at Amnesty that she learned "more about human goodness . . . than [she] had ever known before."

Evil finds expression in the pages of Harry's life as he fights Voldemort, but, paralleling the author's experience, it is never stronger than friendship and love.

Dear Ms. Rowling,

If you were to walk into my house and look very closely at each room, you would notice that they all have one thing in common: books. In scattered piles over tables; stacked precariously over lamps; nestled in bedsheets; hidden under pillows; even in the dark recesses of a late relative's room, stuck under a heater sprinkled with dead termites and bees. And then there are the books that are lucky, old, or reread enough to deserve a shelf. Those are the good ones. The ones that have changed our lives, kept our minds going, or simply had good soufflé recipes. Whether I've read all of them from cover to cover or not, these books are all a part of my life. There are seven of those books in particular which I hold so dear to my heart that it strikes me as odd that their author, whom I admire so much, whom

I feel so close to, is completely unaware of my existence, oblivious to the fact that I have fallen in love with the world she has created.

I first read your books when I was eight years old. For me, that was a time in which I was easily carried away by my imagination, swept off my feet by anything and everything one could find in the fantasy section of my small-town library. So naturally, Harry Potter rendered me speechless: dreaming, hoping, and imagining with all my heart that I would, one day, be whisked away on the Hogwarts Express to this mysterious, beautiful land somewhere in Scotland. But the fact that I read those books — that's not the important part. It's *how* I read them that matters.

For as long as I knew the word *book*, I knew that my father had some choice words to say about quite a few of them. This included Harry Potter. Once he read the review for them in the newspapers, he declared the books Not Allowed. I, knowing no alternative, followed his orders. But that didn't stop my sister.

On a foggy day, we went to the library with an unsuspecting babysitter, the perfect circumstance for doing the Forbidden. We tried to walk casually to the corner in which the books were shelved. Of course, I had no intention of reading the material myself — though I admired my sister for her brave indiscretion, I thought that since I was younger, I would get into more trouble than she would. Also, the thought of doing something Not Allowed intimidated me.

But that same winter, a funny thing happened. My uncle (just as oblivious to the forbidden fascination as my ex-babysitter) sent us the whole Harry Potter boxed set for Christmas. My siblings and I thought it best Not To Tell Dad, so we sat huddled in the orangey glow of our room, feverishly flipping through the pages and giggling at the funny bits (I specifically remember the Weasley twins asking girls to the Yule Ball).

You may wonder why I am telling you this, and it's not to show you that we were disobedient children, nor to say that our father was heartless. I am telling you this to let you know that despite our love and respect for our father, we read about Harry Potter because he gave us Something. Reading those seven books filled my little mind with so much wonder and my heart with so much joy that I found myself raising my butterbeer mug to that brave Boy Who Lived, alongside so many others.

I'm not sure if you knew all this would happen — all the movies, fans, merchandise, and such — simply by writing a handful of books. Sometimes, even I'm not sure why a fictitious orphaned boy gained so much popularity. But then I remember all the tears I have shed while those seven dog-eared books were clutched in my hands; how late I have stayed up, tiptoeing with Harry out of the Gryffindor common room at night; and how close I felt to him, whispering "You'll be okay, Harry" in a small voice as he cried under his covers. Then I remember that Harry Potter was there for me when I felt alone; that whenever I needed to,

I could dive into one of those books and we could live in that magical world until I decided I was okay again. And that's how I know. The second that baby boy appeared on the Dursleys' doorstep, lives were enchanted.

You have given the world a gift, Ms. Rowling. You have given millions of people a friend, an adventure, and a happy ending that never ceases to amaze. So now, I thank you. Thank you for giving a little girl and her siblings someone to admire and dream about. Thank you for teaching the children of this world how magical love is, and most of all, Ms. Rowling, thank you for giving me Harry.

Anne Overton

Animal Farm
GEORGE ORWELL

"To my surprise, your book was a great inspiration
to me — not boring at all."
Abbie Beaver

"Looking back through my work, I see that it is invariably
where I lacked a *political* purpose that I wrote lifeless books
and was betrayed into purple passages, sentences without
meaning, decorative adjectives and humbug generally."

In 1922, without the funds needed to attend university, nineteen-year-old Eric Blair gave up his dream of
becoming a writer, joined the Indian Imperial Police, and
was sent to the English colony of Burma, in Southeast
Asia. Decades earlier, England had annexed Burma as part
of India, but by the 1920s, a nationalist movement within
the colony was lobbying for independence. The Burmese
people hated the imperial police, Blair said. He understood why. The police, as an extension of the government,
controlled the people — and often through cruel methods,
what he called "the dirty work of Empire": "The wretched
prisoners huddling in the stinking cages of the lock-ups,
the grey, cowed faces of the long-term convicts, the scarred
buttocks of the men who had been flogged with bamboos."

After five years, he quit and returned to England to revive his dream of becoming a writer. So as not to embarrass his family, he hid his identity behind a pen name: George Orwell. As Orwell, he wrote *Animal Farm,* a political satire exploring the Russian Revolution and the regime of Joseph Stalin by playing them out in a barnyard.

Dear Mr. Orwell,

I am thirteen years old and in the eighth grade. I like playing sports, listening to music, hanging out with friends, and reading. I think my passion for reading comes from my mother. She always has a book by her side, and her knowledge of events and books is so broad that she amazes me. Until this year, she has allowed me to read any books that interested me, which were mostly fantasy, fiction, and mythology. However, now she has advised me to stretch my reading and challenge myself to read books I might not like. One of those books was *Animal Farm.* She said it was a political book, and my first thought was, *Oh, great, this ought to be good and boring.* To my surprise, your book was a great inspiration to me — not boring at all, and because of your book, I went on to read Martin Luther King's "I Have a Dream" speech and then Anne Frank's *Diary of a Young Girl.*

I feel the most significant impact your book has had on my life was to make me question whether humankind has learned anything from the misery we have caused others. I look around my school and still see how social classification holds people down. I know you are probably saying, "Middle school politics: how childish," but it is at this age where acceptance for who we are is so important. Our confidence depends on it. This is the time in our lives that we are either built up or put down, accepted or rejected, praised or ignored.

I wonder how this social system came about in school, where we are all supposed to be friends. Yet we have our Napoleon and Snowball, always wanting to run everything their way. Then there are always the Bluebells, Jessies, and Pinchers, making sure Napoleon and Snowball get their way by keeping everyone else down. I see that the cheerleaders and jocks get away with lots of things, that the GT (gifted talented) kids are expected to be perfect, and that the students that march to their own drum are made fun of for being different. I want to know why some people feel superior to others just because they might have more money, be a little smarter, have a different heritage, or be blessed not to have any handicaps. Social classification of students and making them feel inferior has to stop. As students, did we not learn anything from the Columbine High School shootings? Apparently not.

After reading *Animal Farm*, I started looking at myself and I really didn't like what I saw. I was one of those who allowed others to pigeonhole me into a group when in reality they didn't know me at all. They didn't really know what interested me, what hurt me, or what I cared about, because I never let them in for fear of rejection. I walked around guarded, fitting in with who I was with at the time. Now I realize that I allowed myself to be a victim. If I want social classification to stop, it has to start with me.

I challenge myself to join clubs that aren't popular but that I like. I will become active in things I don't excel in and let my voice be heard whether it is politically correct or not. I will not be afraid for people to see me fail, and, above all, I will have the confidence to laugh at my own mistakes. I plan to continue to accept people for who they are and hope everyone sees each other's value as golden.

I want to thank you and my mother for inspiring me to read more insightful and controversial books. However — with a keen eye for underlying themes — I will continue to read fiction and mythology. After all, variety is the spice of life.

Abbie Beaver

Bridge to Terabithia
KATHERINE PATERSON

"Queen of Up, Up"
Arielle Moosman

"She was bright, imaginative, and funny. She laughed at his jokes and he at hers. She was the only girl daring enough to invade the second-grade boys' T-ball team."

Katherine Paterson could have been talking about Leslie Burke, one of the main characters in *Bridge to Terabithia*, but she was talking about Lisa Hill, her son's best friend in the second grade. One August morning, the phone rang with tragic news. Lisa had died after being struck by lightning. Katherine's son struggled with Lisa's death, believing that somehow he had been bad and God had punished him by taking Lisa away. Katherine also struggled, and her grief helped her write *Bridge to Terabithia*. Her first draft was a cry of anguish. At first, she could not write what she has called "the fatal chapter," in which Leslie dies, because it meant losing Lisa all over again. But she did write it. And then her editor asked a simple question: Was this a story of friendship or of death?

Friendship, Katherine said. And then she began to rewrite.

Dear Ms. Paterson,

   Bridge to Terabithia has changed my view of the world by reminding me that you can be anything you want. It also taught me to take joy in everything and that even bullies like Janice Avery might not be so bad. They might even need a little help at times. In my own life, I can relate to Leslie feeling left out in school. I was homeschooled until fourth grade, and it has been difficult going to public school. My family lived in a national monument for twelve years, and now we live off the grid. Like Leslie, we don't have TV. We don't miss it. I've always stayed busy exploring, building forts, visiting my tree friends, and having adventures with my dogs. Since I started going to school, there is less time at home. My imagination has been stifled, bit by bit.

   But as I started to read *Bridge to Terabithia*, it was like greeting an old friend. My mind opened up the old, dusty, long-forgotten vaults that held my imagination. I know that this book really changed my view of the world because I have started to see again. I'm starting to regain my imagination and live in another world now. It is almost like I have been given a new pair of eyes. Now I can see how I saw when I was small, before I went to school and went through what I call the "Imagination Bottling Plant." Part of it is growing up, but I think it is very important to keep our imagination wild and free, to believe that anything is possible. I feel like you wrote this book just for me. Thank you!

I know that you can't take anything for granted in life. Leslie's life was so short. Jess was angry with himself because he felt he could have prevented her death. But he realized that Leslie had given him a valuable gift. The best way to keep Leslie alive in his heart was to give the gift away, so he built the bridge to Terabithia and took May Belle by the hand to usher her into the wonderful place called Terabithia. The giving of a valuable gift doesn't diminish the gift; it multiplies it. I can relate to this in my own life because I have lost a grandfather, a grandmother, and my "best dog in the world" in the last few years.

Ms. Paterson, as I close, I want to thank you for the character of Leslie Burke. I guess that I should really be thanking Lisa Hill, who inspired her character. They both gave me so much. Every day as I walk into school, I don't drag my feet as I once did. I say to myself, "All right. Today, no matter how much the other kids tease you about not having a TV, or a brother or sister, not having friends, or just being different, you are going to be like Leslie and Lisa. You are going to look life square in the face with a heart full of imagination." That has helped me so much. I would like to share with you a poem that I wrote when I was three years old (I told it to my mom and she typed it). It is about where I live, my special place called Up, Up. It reminds me of Leslie's Terabithia. It's something small that I can give back to you, to thank you for the wonderful story, and for reminding me that I, too, am a queen.

Up, Up

My world is a happy place!

I have a special bridge that my dad made me. There's no
    water now.

How will we get the water back?

Wait for the snow. Wait for the rain. Wait for the spring.

I like my special world because the ladybugs are there.

We go fishing in the mud . . . for pretend fish.

I got one! I got one!

We laugh in the warm sun.

Yours in Terabithia,
Arielle, Queen of Up, Up

The Diary of a Young Girl
ANNE FRANK

"Because, dearest Anne, because
your Kitty understands."
Jisoo Choi

After her years in the Secret Annex writing in her diary, which she addressed as Kitty, Anne Frank became one of the more than a million children who died in Nazi concentration camps during World War II. She died in Bergen-Belsen from typhus just weeks before the Allied troops liberated the camp at the end of the war.

Anne's diary might have been lost forever except for two women: Miep Gies and Bep Voskuijl. When Anne and her family were in hiding, these two women were among those who helped them by providing food, clothes, books, and news from the outside world. After the Nazis discovered the secret apartment and arrested the two families living in it, Gies and Voskuijl returned to it. Scattered over the wooden floor of one of the rooms were Anne's diaries, including an autograph book with a red-and-white plaid cover and three hundred loose pages. The women gathered the papers and Gies slipped them into a desk drawer, hoping that one day Anne would return. But of the Frank family, only Anne's father, Otto, survived the concentration camps. After the war, Gies gave him his daughter's papers, calling them Anne's legacy.

Dear Anne,

I hold your diary in my hands, and I feel as if you are speaking to me from years past. You are telling me how much it annoys you that the van Daans are always quarreling. You're whispering sadly that you think you will never become close with your mother. Your scream rings in my ear, and the echo tells me you are tired of crying yourself to sleep. And it tears my heart in half. Thank you for speaking to me. Thank you for your diary. Thank you for your legacy you have left for the world, for me.

I am thirteen years old, the same age you were when you first went into hiding, the same age you were when you set foot into the solitary world you would know for over two years. And at such a young age, your dreams have inspired so many all over the world. And because of you, I have learned not to wait until I am older to achieve my dreams, not to think about "When I grow up, I will . . ." but to strive to inspire at my age, just as you have. The fact that you have become an amazing, worldwide inspiration both comforts and challenges me.

Reading your account of the two years you spent in hiding, I cried with you, learned with you, dreamed with you. I came to know you and came to appreciate you for who you were. You cried to me so many times about how your family can't love you for being you. If only you had known that your diary would be published for the world to be inspired by. . . . If only you had known that the "musings of a thirteen-year-old schoolgirl" that you thought nobody would want to read, made such a difference for another thirteen-year-old schoolgirl. Anne, in the beginning of your diary, you wrote that you did not have your one true friend. And throughout the progression of your diary, you continuously wished that you could have a friend to confide all your sorrows and aspirations in. That was Kitty.

You thought that the only person reading your letters would be you. Your letters so filled with fantasies one day and frustrations the next. But, Anne, the world has become your Kitty. I have become your Kitty. And I am so grateful.

Every time there's a disagreement or commotion in the Secret Annex, you always come back to your diary. You even wrote once, "When I write I can shake off all my cares. My sorrow disappears, my spirits are revived!" As an aspiring writer, just like you, I also find solace in writing. I have school notebooks filled with fragments of ideas for stories, planners with a poem on every other page. But, like you again, I also wonder if I really have talent, worry if I'll ever be able to write something great. I worry about the same things as you, and although you may have thought they were petty concerns, they're everything I challenge myself to overcome. And reading your unabashedly honest and real narrative, I found a real friend in you.

As a girl reading your diary over a half a century since you penned it, I know the ending to your story. And I'm sorry you had to face such injustice. Those who live the most deserving lives always seem to be silenced so unfairly and so brutally. You dreamed so ardently of the days after the war. You wrote yourself to freedom in the space which confined your body but not your soul. I am grateful, for although the world never heard your voice, you have left your words as your story. I've gone through hardships in my life as well, though none have been as trying as your years in the Annex, and I've gone through them by writing and dreaming my way out, just as you have those long two years. You dared to dream, in spite of the reality that threatened you daily, and you have allowed me to dream as well. You are truly a role model to me.

You have shown me the subtle beauties in life. You have let me experience the sheer power of words, the words that connect generations across the globe. You have left a spark in my heart that will kindle the flames of hope in my darkest days. Whenever I despair, or consider giving up, your voice will be whispering your dreams and hopes, because they are mine also. Anne, you needn't worry those times when you felt no one understood. Because, dearest Anne, because your Kitty understands.

Jisoo Choi

The Book Thief
Markus Zusak

"For the first time in my life, I found a part of the German nation with which I could sympathize."
Bertina Kudrin

For three years, Markus Zusak wrote and rewrote and still couldn't seem to get the story he was working on quite right. "I tried first person, third person, second person, shifting points of view, present and past tense, and none of it gave me what I wanted."

The story was set in Germany during the Holocaust, and the main character, Liesel, was based on the author's mother. His parents were children in Munich during World War II and later immigrated to Australia. Markus remembers sitting in the kitchen with his brother and two sisters listening to his parents' stories of wartime Germany. Two of his mother's memories stayed with him: how the sky over Munich burned red during the Allied bombing raids, and how a boy was beaten for offering a starving Jewish man a piece of bread.

Liesel had soon taken on a life of her own, but not until Zusak hit upon the idea of Death as the narrator did all the pieces of the puzzle begin to come together. He understood that Death could be a bit more human.

Dear Mr. Zusak,

I used to be afraid. I used to wake up screaming and seeing a yellow star sewn onto my clothing. I have read many books about the Holocaust, but none of them struck me like *The Book Thief*. Instead of pain and fear, it is a book that focuses on courage, kindness, the power of words, and hope.

My parents told me about the Holocaust at a much younger age than most children learn about it. I was in second grade at the time. Telling me the story was difficult for them. My mother's face was contorted with pain and fear. As Jews, my family has always identified with the Jews who were killed during the Holocaust. As my mother talked that day, she felt something I would not understand until years later. It was a fiery rage at a nation who had sentenced Jews to humiliation, starvation, torture, and death, simply because they were Jewish. It was a struggle to understand *how* people could condemn innocent children to such a fate, and it was, quite simply, fear. For her and the rest of my family, it was easy enough to imagine waking up one day and finding themselves in the camps.

Despite the decades that have passed since the Holocaust, I can never forget the anger that I feel when I think of the German nation. It is a fact that I am ashamed of, and fundamentally represents the prejudice that led to the Holocaust. *The Book Thief* drastically changed my point of view.

Your book showed me a different Germany. It showed

me a little girl, around my age, clinging to books while the world around her shifted in ways she could not control. It showed me a struggling woman fighting to save a sick Jew. It showed me a man who risks everything he loves for the sake of a young Jewish man, and for the first time in my life, I found a part of the German nation with which I could sympathize. There was despair on both sides of the war. Millions were dying in camps, but ordinary German citizens were also killed by bombs. Although I could still imagine myself in the crowd of Jews marching to Dachau, I could also identify with a non-Jewish German girl named Liesel. She was my age and loved books with the same fierceness as I do. She saw the evil of the Nazis and felt the anger I feel. Most of all, she was a child like me. We both love, laugh, cry, and shake with terror. Your book also showed me the true power of words. Words can be uplifting or damning. The Führer used propaganda to influence an entire nation. According to him, Jews were the ultimate enemy. They stole businesses. They corrupted children. They were greedy. They were weak. They were scum.

With each book she steals, however, the book thief saves herself. While Hitler used words to kill, she uses them to save. She finds hope in typed pages, and she gives that hope to others as she sits reading in a bomb shelter.

In the end, *The Book Thief* is different from any other Holocaust book, because of that hope. After Papa, Mama, and the rest of Himmel Street's residents die, I am nearly blinded by sadness, but strangely I am also filled with courage. I see Liesel standing in the rubble, her face streaked with tears but her eyes filled with determination, and I know that some good will always survive.

Over the past two years, I have changed dramatically. As I look at Israel, at that tiny country thriving in a desert, I am filled not with fear but with pride. Two years ago, I hated who I was and hid my identity, terrified of another holocaust. Today I am proud of my people. I am proud to be part of a nation that has survived and risen above the labels it was once branded with.

Your book has changed me in many ways. It has given me sympathy, pride, and hope. Therefore, as I flip through the pages of your novel, I am overcome with a flurry of emotions and a realization: the choice is up to me. I can fear the Holocaust, and I can fear who I am. I can be angry at innocent people, and I can look at this time in history and see only darkness, despair, and misery. But I can also see hope. I can see the kindness and selflessness hidden in the depths of two silver-colored eyes. I can see the pride and strength of a girl with soft, feathery hair. Most of all, I can see the book thief in all her glory, standing among the ruins of heaven and knowing that one day, somehow, she will find a way to smile again.

Your faithful reader,
Bertina Kudrin

Maus
ART SPIEGELMAN

"All students learn differently."
Jonathan Hoff

Art Spiegelman is not particularly fond of the term *graphic novel*. He prefers the word *comix* to describe what he does. Comix stem from an underground movement begun in the 1950s that used the forms of comic strips and comic books to focus on more adult themes and images. Reacting to the phrase *graphic novel* applied to his work, Spiegelman says, "It's not like I want it all dressed up in a tuxedo so it can be in public." But he adds that if that's what it takes to get people to read the genre, then, "so be it."

His book *Maus* was the first graphic novel to win the Pulitzer Prize. As much about the author's relationship with his father as it is about the horror of the Holocaust, *Maus* is based on interviews with Spiegelman's father, who survived Auschwitz. Spiegelman's mother, Anja, also survived the Holocaust but took her own life when Art was twenty years old.

Dear Art Spiegelman,

History. Not my favorite subject throughout middle school. Mesopotamia, King Tutankhamen, Julius Caesar — I cannot really relate to these topics; I find these subjects rather boring. I have found my interest in history nonexistent. Sometimes I just do not understand the "why" part of history. For example, why have people throughout history fought so much? Why is there such prejudice in the world? How come there have been world wars but not world peace? There are just too many "whys" for me that cannot be explained. The way the material is presented in school has also been a problem for me. I have a severe visual disability and find it very difficult to follow along in a book and track the words. History books are usually huge and have a plethora of words written on each page. This is problematic for me and, unfortunately, my interest in history has dwindled over the years due to these issues.

Your book *Maus* has changed my relationship with history, has changed the way I look at history, and has changed the way I view my world. I am in eighth grade and have struggled for years with reading books for school due to my disability. I am legally blind in one eye and also have other visual difficulties. If there are too many words on a page, my eyes cannot track the information and I lose interest. It is too overwhelming for me. I turned to art and drawing as a way to relieve my anxiety. I have been known to doodle all through my middle-school classes. Taking cartooning classes has helped me hone my skills and show emotion and movement with my drawings. I do my best doodling during math and social studies. My teachers may not appreciate my artwork, but art and drawing are ways for me to relax, focus, and learn.

When I learned our eighth-grade Language Arts class was going to read your book *Maus* and that it was a graphic novel about the Holocaust, I have to admit I was intrigued and relieved that it was not just any other history book. How could such a serious topic be presented in a comic-book format? I thought about the prejudices during that time period against Jewish people and I could not fathom how an author could possibly present this serious topic through the use of a graphic novel. A comic book about the Holocaust? How could it be possible? You, Mr. Spiegelman, made this concept possible.

Your novel *Maus*, because it was written in a graphic-novel format, made me understand the atrocities of World War II and the hatred the Germans had for the Jewish people in a way I could understand and appreciate. Characters are depicted as animals, which makes it very easy for the reader to identify the subjects. Using mice, cats, and pigs to tell a serious, historical, and personal story makes me believe there is hope for me to one day love history. The panels on each page brought your father's story of his experience during the Holocaust to life. The surprise of finding your private comic book about your mother's suicide within this graphic novel about the Holocaust was courageous. I never expected to find such a personally tragic event in an already tragic account. The distortions and exaggerations of the settings drawn within the panels showed me mood and tone that I would have never gotten from the written words. The illustrations truly affect the novel in a powerful and commanding way.

Furthermore, your book has proven to me that all students learn differently. Not every student has the ability to read a book, memorize the information, and take a test. How much information is actually retained when learning in this manner? For me, not much. The way the material is presented to the student can make a huge difference in what the student retains. Your story of your personal experience and of your family's experience during and after the Holocaust affected my life in a positive way. The book did this by using illustrations to help me to learn more about history and about how history shapes our future. Students are not all made from the same "cookie cutter." We learn differently because we are all different. Students need to be inspired by being exposed to different ways of thinking, and your book has done that for me. *Maus* has helped me to understand a very difficult and horrific part of history. Your book has also inspired me to use my writing and drawing talents to inspire others.

Jonathan Hoff

Lord of the Flies
WILLIAM GOLDING

"I felt a twinge of fear at what I could become."
Kara S. Moritz

"I had discovered what one man could do to another," William Golding said of his time in the British Royal Navy during World War II. Greed and sadistic violence overruled intelligence and compassion. "Anyone who moved through those years without understanding that man produces evil as a bee produces honey, must have been blind or wrong in the head."

After the war, Golding returned to his prewar job as a teacher. But he was no longer the young man he had been, someone who believed that man was capable of creating a perfect society based on goodwill. Haunted by his war experience and his knowledge of the boys he taught, he wrote *Lord of the Flies*, an exploration of humans' inhumanity. Seven publishers rejected the novel. The editor who was eventually responsible for publishing it had retrieved it from the rejection pile. Golding wrote many books and actually considered *Lord of the Flies*, which became a widely read classic, to be one of his lesser works. He expressed regret at its having been published at all because it overshadowed what he thought was his better work.

Dear Mr. William Golding,

Before I knew the true meaning of *Lord of the Flies*, I called it fiction. But when I read about the fire being set to the hillside and Jack breaking Piggy's glasses, *Lord of the Flies* became more than a mere fictional book and far closer to reality than I cared to admit.

When the news channel lists in silence those lost in the war, my family usually stops whatever we're doing to stand at attention. One evening during the time that I was reading *Lord of the Flies*, the faces flashed on the screen and I considered: "Is the war in Iraq truly any different from *Lord of the Flies*?" It is simply *Lord of the Flies* on a larger scale. "How can this be?" I asked myself. "How can humans do this to one another?" I wish I knew the answer, but preventing such things is about as easy as it is for Ralph to stop Jack.

One day during silent reading as I witnessed, as a reader, the horrific killing of the sow, I glanced up for a moment, attempting to absorb the sheer terror of it, and my eye caught something happening among the reading students scattered in corners and across the floor. I saw a pencil fly through the air, landing among a group of kids. Then it was followed by another. Return fire was sent, accompanied by giggles and laughter. "It starts here," I realized. Today it is just good clean fun. But when this escalates, fun turns into desire, desire into want. And want turns into urge, just as it does in *Lord of the Flies*.

When civility fades, who is to say that something more

will not come of such things? I glanced warily back down at the words spinning back at me. I felt my pulse a little stronger, my forehead a little warmer, and my fragile control over instincts slipping. In that moment, I realized how close I was to someone from *Lord of the Flies*. I felt myself identifying with not just Piggy and Ralph, but all of the terrible others as well. I knew that each of them had a corner inside me, held back by a glass wall that I knew would cut me if they shattered it. I saw all of them reflected in each of us, and I felt a twinge of fear at what I could become.

After reading *Lord of the Flies*, something fundamental within me stirred. I have been unable to regain the ignorant tranquility that this place within me had before. I obtained recognition for the shadows of reality and the depths of what appears on the surface. Before reading, I knew only a fragile surface of life. It is as if I can see a reflection previously invisible to me.

Another thing that your book taught me is to stand up for my ideas and opinions. Ralph makes the error of letting Jack get out of control. *Lord of the Flies* reminds me to stand up to the Jack in my life before he goes too far. Sometimes I feel somewhat out-of-the-loop with all my friends, because they have Facebook accounts or cell phones or whatever, but now I have learned that I would rather be out-of-the-loop than subject to the changing voices of the latest social networking fad. Just like those who followed Jack, Facebook and things like that lead to a group mind, which can result in dramatic consequences.

Now I am content with not knowing what my friends are talking about in exchange for freedom from a *Lord of the Flies* reality. Your book helped me to understand this.

After reading your book, I began to acknowledge who I really am, and what lies dormant inside me. I know that a situation like *Lord of the Flies* is unacceptable, as is the greater conflict in the world today. *Lord of the Flies* reminds me not to let the Jacks in my life control me, and to prevent islands from being set aflame today. It reminds me to keep my choir cap on, the conch in hand, and to never let Jack or any of his followers come through in my life.

Kara S. Moritz

Fahrenheit 451
Ray Bradbury

"Keeping a leash on the minds of school-age children"
Shannon Chinn

"I wasn't worried about freedom," Ray Bradbury said of *Fahrenheit 451*. "*Fahrenheit* is not about censorship. It's about the moronic influence of popular culture through local TV news, the proliferation of giant screens and the bombardment of factoids."

Bradbury wrote *Fahrenheit 451* in the typing room in the basement of the library at the University of California at Los Angeles. The machines cost a dime for a half hour. Bradbury did not have many dimes to spare: he had a family to support and a book to write. So he worked quickly, frantically, in beat with the ticking clock, dropping dime after dime. He finished the first draft of the science-fiction novel in nine days. It cost him $9.80.

The irony was not lost on him: in a library, he had created a novel about a future in which books are burned.

Dear Ray Bradbury,

I *love* to read. Books are a part of my life I never want to let go. Your book *Fahrenheit 451* made me realize how great of a possibility we have of books being banned and gone for good. In your depiction of future America, books are burned by firemen at the temperature of 451 degrees Fahrenheit. The thought of the works of my favorite authors being destroyed and forgotten, regarded as dangerous, touched me to the core. It is a future I do not even want to consider, but yet we are already seeing resemblances between our present and your future. More and more, you see fewer and fewer people picking up books and instead picking up iPods, TV remotes, and the newest smartphones. Me, being a part of the teenage era, have of course come across this. Technology is a part of modern life now, and you showed us a glimpse of this in your book by the "parlor families" and "Fun Parks," your version of our electronic entertainment. This ever-growing-larger aspect of life isn't a problem — until it grows so big that it swallows everything else, such as simple paperback and hardcovers seeming to need to be replaced by the newest Nooks and Kindles. Will there come a time when paper books stop being printed at all?

Fahrenheit 451 has also made me realize something I never acknowledged about literature. Lately, you see books banned from schools and libraries due to whatever reason. Parents complain that books such as *Adventures of Huckleberry Finn* and *To Kill a Mockingbird* should not be taught to their children due to profanity and "racial slurs." Even books like *Bridge to Terabithia* and the Harry Potter series develop controversy because of themes of witchcraft and disrespect toward adult figures. Harry Potter is one of my (and thousands upon millions of others') all-time favorite book series. Imagine if these books and many others were never read at all because some people thought they were not appropriate. "Colored people don't like *Little Black Sambo*. Burn it. White people don't feel good about *Uncle Tom's Cabin*. Burn it. Someone's written a book on tobacco and cancer of the lungs? The cigarette people are weeping? Burn the book." This is what Captain Beatty says about the censorship of literature. Books are meant to be debated, conversed about, and argued about, not thrown out due to clashing ideas of what should or should not be available to the world. Reading *your* book made me think about this: the reasons for authors putting profanity in their books are their own, perhaps as a counterexample of the morals the book is trying to impart or however it may be explained, but their work shouldn't be hidden away from the public eye or burned away as an illegal item.

I think that one of my favorite parts of your book is the large spectrum of characters. I see the characters as a portrayal of different aspects of the story. Clarisse McClellan, for example, is the person who starts to change Guy Montag's way of thinking. "Is it true that long ago firemen put fires *out* instead of going to start them?" "Do you ever *read* any of the books you burn?" "Are you happy?"

These questions asked by Clarisse seemed to linger with Guy throughout the book and fuel his actions of rebellion toward the censorship and burning of books. Guy begins as a simple-minded member of society, like everyone else, acting as a dutiful fireman: "It was a pleasure to burn." What we end with is a man who has lost everything, for books and literature and knowledge, while the rest of the citizenry sits and watches the parlor walls, wasting their lives away and becoming disconnected, like Margaret, Guy's wife, who spends more time with her "parlor family" than with her own husband.

These points in the story got me thinking. What kind of people will our society and our generation choose to become as the days between our time and yours grow shorter? Are we going to decide to ask the questions "why" not "how" like Clarisse, or will we turn into the mindless characters of your future America, people who don't bother to break the barrier between what they do and don't know, leaving what's left on the other side to be burned and forgotten? I've never even thought about any of this before picking up your book.

Fahrenheit 451 made me realize things that I had never managed to pull from my seventh-grade mind. Is technology becoming such a big influence on our teenage generation that it will replace books altogether? Is censorship in schools becoming a bigger burden on literature, keeping a leash on the minds of school-age children, middle-schoolers like me, and preventing them from reading important books in our history or just excellent books in themselves? How far until our present becomes your future? Does our society really mirror yours so closely? All these questions came up in my mind while reading and wholeheartedly devouring your book. Thank you, Mr. Ray Bradbury, for making me realize how precious books and reading are, and how we should cherish our literature. Thank you for making me realize how much technology influences me, and pretty much all of modern America. Thank you for giving me the experience of a lifetime reading your book. I've never loved reading more.

Sincerely,
Shannon Chinn

Speak

LAURIE HALSE ANDERSON

"For the first time, I heard my own silence."
Emmy Goyette

"Literature is a fantastic way to learn about the kinds of hardships you may have to deal with; watching characters grow and change is a great way to strengthen yourself for your own challenges," states Laurie Halse Anderson. Her novel *Speak* deals with a controversial subject: rape. The author calls the book "a cautionary tale."

As she tells it, one night, she dreamed of a girl screaming for help. She hurried into her daughters' bedrooms to be certain they were fine. They were. But the sudden bolt of waking from the dream left her wired. She has been plagued by nightmares throughout her life and often writes in her journal to find solace and be able to fall back asleep. That night the dream triggered an idea for a book: *Speak*, about a young woman's grief, isolation, and guilt after being raped. The protagonist, high-school freshman Melinda, was raped over the summer and hasn't spoken to anyone about it. It'll take brain surgery, she says, to cut the memory of it out of her head.

The book received much praise, but some parents and educators objected to the sexual content and the book has been the target of censorship. In the years since its publication, thousands of young women have written letters thanking Laurie Halse Anderson for writing Melinda's story and helping them to confront their own painful memories.

Dear Laurie Halse Anderson,

Your book made me realize I needed help.

Even before I had reached page 1 of the story, even before I met Melinda, your book *Speak* was trying to tell me something. Reading the introduction, reading all the letters you received from people who had gone through the same thing, people who had experienced equally horrible things. I found it surprising that I could relate to them. I was having one of my good days, and I was used to the feeling of thinking I was feeling fine. I was fine. I read on.

I read about Melinda's silent struggle. I read about the lip biting and the isolation she felt in school and with her family. I read on as Melinda silently spiraled into her depression. And I could relate. I'm loud. I have friends. I am vocal in class and come across as energetic. I certainly haven't gone through the same thing Melinda did. How could I be feeling the same thing? I was fine. I am fine.

Then I took a closer look at myself. I saw the chewed, raw lips and the tired eyes. I felt the aches, and migraines, and the lost interest in things I used to love. I felt the isolation from the people I used to care about. I felt the emptiness. I felt blank. For the first time, I heard my own silence.

But I've always been a happy person. I was fine.

When Melinda cut her wrists, that's when I really saw it. I saw from a fictional mother the response that I was fearing from my real mother. I saw the ignorance and ridicule I feared from my peers. I saw the fear that had kept me pushing my feelings down for almost a year now. I took a moment to take inventory of my own condition.

Feeling like throwing up when picked for a solo, or when expected to speak in class, is not a normal reaction. Not everybody feels like crying all the time, yet too empty to actually do it. Not everybody hates themselves for no reason. Not everybody wakes up with a pit in their stomach. Not everybody feels smothered and suffocated by their own pointless guilt. Not everybody has indulged in fantasies of pills going down their throat.

I'm loud, but nothing I say means anything. I have friends, but I am so alone. I'm vocal in class, but petrified to make the wrong move. Any form of judgment throws me into a spiral. I'm just so tired.

I need to speak. But will anyone listen? Everybody's gone through something, and I really don't feel like I'm worth enough to compare. My wrists are clean and my laugh is loud. I am not Melinda. The days I look sad pass. The days I feel blank don't. At the same time, Melinda and I are the same. I need to speak, but the right words won't come. Even if they did, would anybody take me seriously, or would I just be another dramatic teenager with an angst struggle? Maybe that's what I am. Maybe I am fine.

But now at least I know that maybe I'm not fine. Now I know I should speak.

I should speak to the friends who have told me their similar struggles, whom I've taken seriously enough to console. I should speak to them for comfort. I shouldn't fear their judgment, their disgust, their exasperation at just another exaggerated teenage sob story.

I should speak to the people that I look down on and see how my words impact them. I should speak so I don't hurt someone without knowing.

I should speak to the people who look down on me, to see if their smiles are plastered on or if their judgment is just backlash. I should speak to forgive.

I should speak to my family, speak without cringing, speak without always feeling awkward, because I want them to know. I want someone to know. I have so much speaking to do, but so much reluctance.

I was so mad at Melinda. I was so upset at her that she wouldn't say anything to anyone, that she wouldn't try to be heard. In my anger at your character, I realized I should be feeling the same anger toward myself. I hope to take inspiration from Melinda's courage to cry out. I hope to take control of myself, and my words. I hope I'll be fine.

Emmy Goyette

Steve Jobs
Walter Isaacson

"It was uncomfortable to look into his world
and see the pain."
Gabriel Ferris

Is genius intelligence a high IQ? Or is it an alternative way
of viewing the world, looking to the future and imagining
the possibilities of what could be and then achieving the
vision? Walter Isaacson's biographies explore the breadth
of genius: Benjamin Franklin's knowledge, ranging "from
science to government to diplomacy to journalism"; Albert
Einstein's imagination as "he tried to picture what it would
be like to ride alongside a light beam"; and Steve Jobs's
"imaginative leaps," the way "like a pathfinder, he could
absorb information, sniff the winds, and sense what lay
ahead."

Dear Walter Isaacson,

For the last few years I have been obsessively interested in computers, especially Macs. I picked up a copy of
your book about Steve Jobs, excited by the thought that
I might find a few technical nuggets that could broaden

my horizons. I learned nothing about technology by reading your book but rather received an unintended lesson on
the delicate tightrope that often divides extreme business
success and extreme failure in personal relationships.

Like so many highly successful people, Steve Jobs was
driven by something that not many people have. This special something is called singular focus. As a result, Jobs had
the ability to focus on only one thing and to tune out everything that didn't align with his goal. Throughout this book
I found myself questioning if Steve's high level of business
success was worth the price he paid on a personal level.

Many a teenager in the twenty-first century would
like nothing more than to be Steve Jobs, the founder of
one of the largest, coolest businesses in the world! This
was true about me until the day I flipped open the cover
of your book. Reading about his rags-to-riches story that
started in his garage was inspirational and entertaining.
However, overshadowing all this was the mess he made
of his personal life — and even some relationships in his
business life. At times I felt bad for those around him. It
was uncomfortable to look into his world and see the pain
caused by his behavior.

Despite these feelings, I couldn't put the book down.
You brought me into his world in a way that no other book
has. It inspired me. The reason your book inspired me was
that it taught me that failing from taking risks in business
(Jobs's computer Lisa) is not bad. Your writings actually
taught me that risk-taking as well as failing can be good to

the extent that you learn from your mistakes. This concept that failing can be ultimately productive played out many times in your story of Steve's life.

Additionally, I was inspired by examples of what I don't want to be. It showed me that true singular focus can be very expensive in terms of human relationships. Steve Jobs was so focused on his singular goal that he ignored some of the most important things in his life — family and friends. Steve went so far as to not see his girlfriend with whom he had a daughter. When reading this part of your book, I had to go back and reread this section because it seemed so surreal to me that a person could actually say no to seeing his own daughter or being part of her life. When putting myself in Steve's position, I could never imagine doing something as extreme as this. I found myself asking if this behavior was normal for Silicon Valley executives. Is the value of family life typically lost in the pursuit of the Silicon Valley dream?

This same singular focus that interfered with family life also contributed to failed relationships at work. Steve Jobs had a single vision, and he wasn't generally open to deviations. As I read his story, I realized that he wasn't anyone I'd want to work for! His coworkers complained that he was too determined and in fact acted like an unpredictable small child when he didn't get what he wanted. A perfect example of this was when Steve worked at Atari. His inability to work with others had him restricted to work hours when no one else was around. When I first read the chapter about his days at Atari, I didn't really understand how someone could be too determined, too driven, and too rigid. It was not until many chapters later that I started to realize that the same factors that played into his extreme success were the very factors that contributed to his personal human failure in almost all relationships. I remember a point where I stopped reading to try to pull my thoughts together as my vision of what I thought was a model life story was falling apart.

It's only been a month or so since I finished your book on Steve Jobs. I still think about it a few times a week. You changed my life in a way I didn't anticipate. I'm conflicted about the price of success. At thirteen years old, I haven't read a lot of biographies that detail the personal lives of super-successful people. I understand that an underlying theme for the super-successful is being fully dedicated to the goal at hand. Steve Jobs's behavior reminds me of Oscar Wilde's comment that "nothing succeeds like excess." Is excess a requirement for extreme success? Your story leaves me wondering if this is the case — and struggling with the balance between wanting to do something great while still being someone great. Consequently, your story created more questions in my life than it answered.

Gabriel Ferris

The Hobbit
J. R. R. TOLKIEN

"I still imagine my bedroom as a hobbit-hole."
Elizabeth Chambers

"In a hole in the ground there lived a hobbit," wrote J. R. R. Tolkien. At the time he wrote that sentence, Tolkien actually had no idea what a hobbit was. As he began to imagine the story of Bilbo Baggins, he realized that "Hobbits are just rustic English people, made small in size because it reflects (in general) the small reach of their imagination — not the small reach of their courage or latent power."

Tolkien was foremost a linguist and a constructor of languages. The language he created for the setting of Middle-earth, inspired by Finnish, Welsh, and Hebrew, actually preceded the writing of the stories: "the stories were made . . . to provide a world for the languages." While recovering from "trench fever," contracted while fighting in the First World War, he began writing the stories that became *The Silmarillion*, his chronicle of the creation of the universe Eä and its population of elves, men, and dwarves. His son Christopher remembers sitting on a footstool at his father's feet and listening to tales of elves and dwarves in a mythological history of England.

At first Tolkien wrote *The Hobbit* as an independent

children's story, not linked with the greater universe of *The Silmarillion*, but in the process of writing the story, he began to see the connection between Bilbo's Shire and the legends of Middle-earth. The world of the hobbits is not merely a place. Middle-earth has a geography, a history, a language, and a culture and is part of a much larger universe, all imagined and formulated in deep detail.

Dear Mr. Tolkien,

Your extraordinary and literally out-of-this-world novel *The Hobbit* has changed my perspective on the importance and power of change, the importance of being open to new and difficult challenges, and has shown me my inborn courage and confidence to be adventurous. The first time I read your book, I smiled at the last sentence on the 287th page, and I knew this was a book that I would read again and again. Years after I first read it (my mother's own childhood copy, which was published in 1978 and has now been lovingly passed on to me), I still imagine my bedroom as a hobbit-hole, my backyard as Mirkwood, and my dog as the scaly, cunning dragon Smaug.

During the summer, while at my family's cabin in the woods, I often curl up on the couch with a blanket and a book, immersing myself in a new stack from the library, but always going back to *The Hobbit*. My younger brother Oliver would call to me, "C'mon, E! Let's go down to the lake!" I would shake my head and nestle deeper in the paperback world. Your book taught me the simple choice of unexpectedly stepping out your door and running down the path, just as Bilbo Baggins instigates an adventure. After reading your book, when my brother called to me to go outside, I smiled and ran out after him, letting the screen door slam, not bothering with socks or shoes. Flying over the moist soil and dry, scratchy pine needles, and then later trailing our feet in the fresh waters of the lake, I would laugh and say to Oliver, "We're like hobbits, running around barefoot in the mushrooms with our big, hairy feet!"

The summer I turned thirteen, I climbed Fremont Peak, the third tallest mountain in Wyoming, with my family. For eight years my uncle had taken my cousins, brother, and me on various backpacking adventures to prepare us for the final climb. In all my musings of climbing the mountain, I imagined, like in *The Hobbit*, a flame-spewing, gold-lusting dragon living within the caverns of the mountain. I could see in my mind the endless halls and grand, spiraling staircases carved in the granite by stout, bearded dwarves. Most vividly of all, your book helped me visualize myself summiting the mountain, defying my internal urge to stay safely at home with my second breakfast and soft, comfortable bed, and instead going on a life-changing adventure.

At 5:00 a.m., the star-studded sky stretching above Fremont Peak was on the verge of sunrise. As my cousins and I lay curled up in our down sleeping bags, as snug as if we were in our own warm hobbit-holes, our uncle zipped open the tent door and stuck his head in. "Did you hear that?" he said. "That great big noise? That was the crack of dawn!" Reluctantly, I peeled myself off the floor of the tent and crawled out into the dark, cold morning. After four hours of strenuous scrambling up boulder fields and clinging to the cracks and crevices of immense slabs of gray-streaked granite, panting in the thin, high-altitude air, we found ourselves within reach of the top. The diluted blue sky was almost tangible above us as I grunted — muscles burning and protesting, my pack dragging me earth-ward — and clambered onto the summit. The tiny orange fleck of our tent was the only sign of our camp three thousand dizzying feet below. After a deep, emotionally satisfying breath, I grasped a small, gray-blue chunk of mixed quartz and granite between my gloved fingers, and smiling in the face of victory, shouted, "Behold! The Arkenstone!" I packed my treasure seventeen miles out of the mountains, homeward bound, in the top of my thirty-pound pack. To this day the stone rests in a place of honor on my bookshelf, not far from my yellowed, creased copy of *The Hobbit*.

A mere six days after my summit of Fremont Peak, my family moved to Jackson, Wyoming, and I found myself staring wide-eyed at the first day of eighth grade in a new school. Always very shy and acutely aware of myself around others, the prospect of being the new kid was almost overwhelming. But I recalled Bilbo's struggle when a company of dwarves stormed his home and counted on him to join their adventure, and Bilbo's replying yes. I was already signed up for the adventure, and all I had to do was keep dodging the trolls and goblins to find my gold. With clammy, sweating palms, I found a seat in my first class. I turned to introduce myself to the girl sitting in the chair in front of me, took a deep breath, nodding at the book under her chair, and said "What are you reading?"

Every day — during important moments and trivial ones — the world of Middle-earth that you created seems to be so alive and real to me that I feel like I can step in and out of it at will. It is a living, breathing part of me. It is alive in my thoughts, my morals, my pleasures, and my aspirations. As I sit at my desk before a stack of homework, I say to myself in my best imitation of Gollum, "Nasty little homeworkses. We hates them!" When I snatch a pinecone from the forest floor to hurl at a distant outcropping of rock, I imagine it bursts into flame from Gandalf's staff.

Your words and ideas gave me the confidence to climb a mountain, to survive middle school, and to be confident in my success; your words opened my mind to the wonderful effects of adventures. I thank you for what *The Hobbit* has given me: an expanded scope of imagination, and the ability to find enjoyment in changes and challenges instead of shying away from them.

With utmost sincerity,
Elizabeth Chambers

The Lord of the Rings
J. R. R. TOLKIEN

"Gone was the ice skater;
gone were the Olympics."
Ellie Ball

The immediate success of J. R. R. Tolkien's first book, *The Hobbit*, brought pressure from the publishers for a sequel. Tolkien didn't want to write a sequel: he wanted to have his "lost tales" from *The Silmarillion* published, but his editors thought those stories too complex. And so, though it would be seventeen years until it was published, by the end of 1937, Tolkien had begun writing what would become his epic work, *The Lord of the Rings*: "When Mr. Bilbo Baggins of Bag End announced that he would shortly be celebrating his eleventy-first birthday with a party of special magnificence, there was much talk and excitement in Hobbiton. . . ."

Dear J. R. R. Tolkien,

As the wind howls outside and the thunder roars, I sit inside in front of the fireplace, curled up under a blanket, reading a book. I feel like I'm Sam or Frodo, sitting in Bag

End in front of the hearth, listening to Bilbo's stories. But, even though I've read this story too many times to count, each time I unearth something new and surprising about myself. This story is a mirror held up to my face by the hands of fate.

The first time I read *The Lord of the Rings*, I read it for enjoyment. I skimmed the surface like a skater on ice at the Olympics. But the second time, I saw something different. Gone was the ice skater; gone were the Olympics. They were replaced instead with an understanding, the type of understanding that comes with reading the same story again and unearthing a theme beneath all the words.

In *The Lord of the Rings*, Frodo is on a quest to destroy the One Ring and to rid the world of evil and the Dark Lord Sauron. His journey takes him from his home, the quiet, out-of-the-way town of Hobbiton, through Elf dwellings, murky marshes, dark mountain passes, and finally to the very heart of Sauron's evil land and the Mountain of Doom. Frodo meets many people along the way who help and guide him, but above all those people he has his constant companion and best friend, Sam. Sam is always there for Frodo, even when no one else is. His loyalty is incredible. He is always present to encourage Frodo to believe in himself. As I sat, curled up under my blankets, reading the story of Sam and Frodo, I couldn't help but pause, in the very act of turning a page, and think about how Sam and Frodo's friendship compared to the friendships in my own life.

At the time of reading *The Lord of the Rings*, I couldn't say I had a friendship, or at least not a stable one. My friends and I had been divided by some rumors that were circulating about some of us. And, as the ever-so-true saying goes, "Divided we fall." Yes, things weren't going well. There was a lot of internal fighting, gossiping, and rumors going on in my previously stable friendship circle. I was secretly panicking that we'd all go our own ways without even making apologies, and I'd be left alone, without any friends. Reading about Sam and Frodo's friendship helped me realize how to start mending this tear in the fabric of my life.

Friendships are based partly on whether you like someone or not, but mostly on having a shoulder to lean on, a support structure of people who are kind to you and want to see you succeed. This theme is demonstrated many times throughout *The Lord of the Rings*, like when Eowyn and Merry have to work together to kill the Witch-King, or when Sam carries Frodo up the last stretch of their journey to Mount Doom. This kind of support is beautiful because it is done out of goodness of the heart and desire to help another without expecting payment in return. I drew on this to mend my friendship life. I started to encourage people to be nicer and more supportive to everyone in general. I made friends with some girls in my class who didn't have that kind, caring support team that makes life a whole lot easier. One of these girls actually turned out to become one of my very best friends!

But you cannot bring aid to some people sometimes, as sad as that is. You cannot reach out and touch the famine victim from Somalia or the genocide refugee from Rwanda. There is pain and suffering, so much pain and suffering in this world that I only realized it fully after I read your book. I saw the massacres on the plains of Rohan as if I could touch them, and I felt the pain of the loved ones of the victims of the final attempt to retake Osgiliath. It was horrifying, and I made the connection quickly enough to simply drop the book in dumb amazement, staring out my window as if a murderer would come waltzing by any minute.

I decided I wanted to take steps against suffering in my own community. I made bags of old toys in my room to give away, donated coats to the coat drive, and gave food and money to homeless shelters and the food pantry. I'm not pretending that my efforts are making a huge difference in the world, mind you, but it's making a difference in some people's lives, and in mine, and I have learned to treasure that.

Maybe that is the treasure I always know I will find when I open *The Lord of the Rings*. Maybe it's not the adventures, the action, my favorite characters, or my favorite scenes. It's what comes out of the book, the aftermath that lingers in your head that is the real treasure from this book. Now, if you'll excuse me, it's a stormy night, and I've gotten to a particularly good part in my book.

Ellie Ball

To Kill a Mockingbird
HARPER LEE

"It was a hate crime."
Margaret Veglahn

"I want to do the best I can with the talent God gave me," Harper Lee said in a rare interview in 1964, a few years after the publication of her novel *To Kill a Mockingbird*. That novel won the Pulitzer Prize for fiction, and its success overwhelmed the author. Working on a second novel, she said, "I hope to goodness that every novel I do gets better and better."

In 1960, when *To Kill a Mockingbird* was first published, Jim Crow laws in many states still enforced segregation in public places such as theaters, restaurants, bathrooms, and even drinking fountains. The civil rights movement was gaining momentum, but the struggles for civil rights that played out on television broadcasts and in newspaper headlines were frequently marred by violence.

Harper Lee's novel gave America a different picture of racism: the innocence of Scout; the ethical integrity of her father, Atticus Finch; and the dignity of Tom Robinson struck a chord for many readers. The novel was as much about the current struggles for civil rights as it was about the lack of civil rights in a small Alabama town during the 1930s. Even now the novel speaks to the present day as America continues to struggle with civil rights in the twenty-first century.

Dear Harper Lee,

On April 13, 2014, I was preparing to go on for the final performance of a stage adaptation of your book *To Kill a Mockingbird* at the Jewish Community Center of Greater Kansas City. As I was getting my costume on, I heard loud noises coming from the parking lot. We all headed toward the door, but we were stopped and told that under no circumstance were we to leave the building. We waited for what seemed like an eternity as sirens wailed outside. Later that day, the cast was informed that just beyond the wall I was leaning on, two people had been shot and killed. My heart dropped into my stomach.

I looked on the table and saw a copy of your book. I picked it up and flipped to the first page as I had many times before. As my eyes moved from beautiful word to beautiful word, they were opened to what had truly happened just feet away from where I now stood. It was the same thing that happened when Bob Ewell attacked Jem and Scout. It was the same thing that had happened when Tom Robinson was killed in prison. It was a hate crime. The words sent shivers down my spine like when cold air slips silently through your window on a cold winter night.

I found myself unable to stop reading. As I dug deeper and deeper into the story, every word I had read before harnessed a new meaning.

Most people, including myself, assumed that after the Civil Rights Act was passed, hate crimes were no longer an issue. It was while I was knee deep in the trial scene that I understood that hate crimes aren't always about skin color. They can involve religion, political parties, beliefs, and anything else that makes one person different from another. Scout, much like me, was dumbfounded by people who could commit such heinous acts. She went to her father for help. I came to you to guide me through the maze of my thoughts.

I'm trying as hard as I can to find a glimmer of goodness in the man who so nonchalantly murdered two innocent human beings. Those were people with family and friends and jobs and lives. There is nothing more precious than a life. He took them away, and for that I see no glimmer. No goodness anywhere in that heart of steel. As much as your book has changed my view of the world, that is one thing I have a hard time with. Does everyone really have something good in them?

I've read *To Kill a Mockingbird* countless times, trying to sift through my feelings. Each time I discover something I hadn't noticed before. Each time I read the back cover, I stop and talk to the characters in my head. I ask them questions and they talk back. It may seem crazy, but really it's quite therapeutic. I take stock of what I know and what still makes my head spin. No matter how many times I flip the pages of your story, I realize I will never truly be able to let go of the burden that day has put on my life. However, it has been lightened an incredible amount and my back is no longer breaking.

Margaret Veglahn

Night
Elie Wiesel

"I saw my brother Joe try to fight death."
Juliana Gorman

"I swore never to be silent whenever and wherever human beings endure suffering and humiliation," Elie Wiesel said in his acceptance speech for the Nobel Peace Prize. "We must take sides. Neutrality helps the oppressor, never the victim. Silence encourages the tormentor, never the tormented."

Elie Wiesel was fifteen the spring that German soldiers occupied the village of Sighet in Transylvania. Later he remembered how naive the Jewish community was at the time of occupation. They did not believe Nazi Germany would attempt to exterminate the Jewish people. At Auschwitz he and his father were given the "privilege" of being slave laborers. His father did not survive. When Allied troops liberated the camps, Elie was sent to France, one of hundreds of orphaned Jewish children. He was hollow. He had lost his family and his faith.

As an adult, he became a journalist. During an interview with François Mauriac, a French Catholic writer, Wiesel expressed his anguish that the world had known what was happening during the Holocaust but had remained indifferent. Mauriac urged Wiesel to write about what he had experienced in the camps. He did.

Dear Mr. Wiesel,

This year I read your book *Night* for my English class. I attend an all-girls Catholic school, so, as you might imagine, we get assigned a lot of "coming-of-age" books with the main character usually being a teenage girl. When I was assigned your book, I was surprised to find out that a teenage boy was the protagonist. Of course, I naturally wondered what a 2014 Catholic teenage girl in America could have in common with a 1941 Jewish boy in Transylvania. It turns out we share more than you might think.

Early in your book, I realized how important your family was to you. One of your main missions while in the concentration camp was not only to survive, but also to remain with your father. You would find a way to be with him in the infirmary or keep him awake in the cold snowy weather so he would not freeze to death. In the end, you lost your father. Your father had been your will to live. Death was all around you. You saw babies thrown into flames, men marched into the crematoria, men and children hanged right before your eyes. You saw death at a very young age.

Most teenagers never see someone die right before their eyes. I have. I saw my brother die when I was only nine years old. I saw my brother Joe try to fight death just like your father tried to fight. His enemy was not the Germans but the quieter enemy eating away inside him, leukemia. Your book helped me understand some of the things that happened during his hospitalization. For example, my parents would have the whole family attend Saturday-night Mass in the hospital's chapel, then grab food from the cafeteria to eat in my brother's hospital room. Despite the horrible disinfectant smells and gloomy decor, we would laugh so hard as we played board games until visiting hours were over. I now realize that it was important to my parents for us all to be together, regardless of where we were. Just as the concentration camps could not break your bond with your dad, so the leukemia could not stop us from being a family. Those Saturday nights kept us going through two and a half years of hospital stays.

You questioned how and why God was so powerful and almighty but would let such terrible things happen. On Rosh Hashanah, you could not understand how fellow Jews would call God "Blessed." I, too, wondered why God would let my brother die. He was so young, and what could he have done to make God angry? Or was God punishing me or my parents? Surely my brother deserved one of those miracles that my books about saints had spoken of. I felt guilty asking these questions. Your words show me that maybe it is normal to wonder if God is present during hard times. Later, following Joe's funeral, my parents, my other brother, and I continued to go to church. Why should I go and sing praises to Him? Hadn't God abandoned me just like He had abandoned you? I understood why you refused to fast on Yom Kippur. My brother died on Ash Wednesday, and still in the Lenten weeks following his death, my mom refused to serve meat on Fridays. Why should I care about something so silly as not eating meat when God did not care to step in and cure my brother? Again you showed me that it is just part of being human to wonder about these things.

Despite all the confusion inside me, I think your words give me some peace. In your Nobel Prize acceptance speech, you spoke about how we cannot sit by and just let human beings endure suffering. You said that indifference is not acceptable and the only way to fight it is by taking action. Your words motivate me. Each May since my brother's passing, I help at the Join for Joe Bone Marrow Swab Day at my school. At this event, which is named for my brother, I help collect samples of cheek cells, which can help determine if a person is a good match to be a bone marrow donor for a victim of leukemia. Many girls are eager to sign up and hope to be a match. But I have also seen other girls, as well as faculty, try to sneak by the sign-up table outside the cafeteria. They are indifferent. They do not know the suffering you and I have seen. They do not know that one person can make a difference. I will tell them. I will try to make them understand that these random victims of leukemia should not be forgotten. I know one person can make a difference because the Swab

Day found a match last year for a fourteen-year-old girl with leukemia. At age thirteen, I will fight ignorance with the hope of ending more human suffering. Though this is a small drive and we may only collect a hundred swabs, *Night* makes me more committed to this cause.

You speak in *Night* about how you will never forget the smells and sounds and the feelings in the concentration camp. I, too, shall never forget. I will never forget the sad looks of the families in the elevator on the way to the pediatric oncology floor. I will never forget the constant antiseptic smell at home as we tried to keep our house germ free. I will never forget strangers' stares at my brother, who wore his blue baseball cap to cover his hairless head. I will never forget the sick kids on the oncology floor who just wanted to go to school and be like all the other kids. I will never forget these kids and their hope to live. I will never forget my brother Joe.

Juliana Gorman

Thirteen Reasons Why
Jay Asher

"I'm pressing play."
Bailee Stump

"No one reaches out for help if they feel no one will understand," said Jay Asher. "And I've heard over and over that this book was the first time people felt understood." *Thirteen Reasons Why* was Jay Asher's first published novel. He had been writing novels for some time, but this particular book was the first, he has said, in which he felt he had found his writer's voice. The idea for it came, in part, from conversations with a teen relative who shared her pain with him after she had survived a suicide attempt. He wanted to mirror that pain in his protagonist, Hannah, and share his new understanding of how someone gets to the desperate point of trying to end her life.

Thirteen Reasons Why is not just a book about suicide. It is about why suicide can happen. Jay Asher's hope is that the people who read it will find solace and, more important, seek help should they need it or reach out to someone who does.

Dear Jay Asher,

One suicide. Seven cassette tapes. Thirteen reasons. I related to Hannah Baker in ways no one else could. She understood what I was keeping inside me. The hole. This hole eats everything you have: emotions, happiness, and, if you're like Hannah Baker, your life. This hole starts small but it grows based on everything. Hannah Baker understood the hole that lived inside me, but she didn't understand how to stop it.

When I first heard about your book *Thirteen Reasons Why*, I was skeptical. I didn't want to read a book that would be Depression Central, but nevertheless I tried it. Within the first ten pages, I was captive. The idea of a post-suicide story was brilliant, and I got both sides of the situation that I needed: Hannah Baker, the witty girl who was well known, and Clay, the boy who loved her. Hannah wasn't always depressed. Her first reason on the tapes was that Justin, the first boy she kissed, betrayed her even though he was unaware of it. There were many people in my life who were making my own hole grow and were utterly unaware of this damage.

As every day dragged on, I found myself getting a bit gloomier; I found it was getting harder to keep a smile and that it burned to laugh. I spent a lot of time just lying awake at night thinking about life and the things that haunted me. I also didn't talk as much as I used to. I was starting to cut the strings that held me from falling in the hole that was deep inside me and growing a bit larger every day. Simple things would make me feel like shutting down: not being waved back to, unintentionally being excluded from conversations, and hearing about my neighbor's party that I wasn't invited to. These things made the hole devour my heart and I felt worthless until, eventually, I was emotionless or sad all the time. It wasn't the way I had planned on spending my days, but I did. Then Hannah told me that she understood. She knew the pain and emptiness like a sister. She didn't understand why she was living and she, as well as I, was terrified by the future.

Whenever they hear that someone has committed suicide, most people respond with "Bless their family" or something of the sort. My dad would always say, "Suicide is the most selfish thing a person could do." I never understood why he said that until after reading your book. Hannah was so focused on her pain and on her world falling apart that she never saw what she would throw away and who she would hurt when she died. She was so caught up in depression that she did what would benefit no one. She took her own life. This act hurt her parents and friends. She never had the chance to live her life fully because she was examining herself and her problems under a microscope. She never stepped back and took a look at the rest of her life. I learned a lot from Hannah Baker, such as if you don't find the magnificent in the terrible, life becomes nothing more than just going through the motions. I understood her predicament, but I refused to applaud her self-inflicted tragedy.

Hannah Baker didn't find the magnificent in the terrible. She had the reputation of a girl who just gave herself to guys. This was all a rumor due to the first boy she kissed, Justin. He said that he didn't only kiss her — which was a lie — but everyone believed it. This started what Hannah called the "snowball" effect. The more rumors spread about her added speed to this snowball until it grew, and she couldn't stop it. Hannah let the terrible consume her life, and she focused on it like a microscopic cell.

By watching how Hannah let her world fall apart, I looked up from my microscope with my terrible problems, and looked at my life as it is. This is when I found the magnificent. Yes, my mom was on drugs and her rejection of me made me feel like I was worthless, but after cocaine was found in her house, I have been safe with my dad and stepmom. And I'm not worthless. I am loved as if I am my stepmom's own daughter, and my two brothers, even though they can drive me up the wall, look up to me and would be heartbroken if I wasn't there. My "magnificent" is my family — who wouldn't be my family without my "terrible." Seeing Hannah Baker take her life when she still had something to hold on to made me realize that in any situation of terrible there is some magnificent and that taking your own life because you can't see that others love you, because you're focused on yourself, is selfish.

Hannah then stopped her future. I'm pressing play.
Bailee Stump

· PART THREE ·
HIGH SCHOOL

"I Am Not a Nobody"

LETTERS ABOUT LITERATURE

"I am not a nobody. I may not be the most popular person, or the most good-looking. I'm not the person everyone goes to for advice. I am more like that person everyone comes crying to when everything has gone wrong. They say, 'No one was there for me!' And I say, 'I was.' I try to make myself pretty, but nobody notices. Some of my friends don't even notice. They are there for me . . . sometimes."

—Sarah Griffith in a letter to Amanda Hocking about her book *Switched*

Two Old Women
VELMA WALLIS

"Courage to conquer my fears"
Anna Marie Wichorek

According to an Athabascan legend, two aging women had become a burden to their community. They no longer contributed to the welfare of the village and relied on others for food and shelter. When the villagers moved to their winter camp, they left the two old women behind. Death seemed inevitable, but the abandoned women did not die. They remembered their old skills — how to trap and hunt and weave rabbit fur into clothing. They remembered which plants to dig from under the snow to eat.

Velma Wallis is of Athabascan descent. When she was a girl, her mother told her this legend. "I was impressed with it," she later wrote, "because it not only taught me a lesson that I could use in my life, but also because it was a story about my people and my past — something about me that I could grasp and call mine."

When she was a young woman, Velma left her family to live in an isolated trapping cabin in the interior region of Alaska near the Yukon River, just miles from the Arctic Circle. She lived independently as her people had for generations, trapping and hunting her own food. And she wrote *Two Old Women: An Alaska Legend of Betrayal, Courage, and Survival.*

Dear Velma Wallis,

Last year, my eighty-four-year-old grandfather moved in with our family. Along with him came a wheelchair, a walker, a box full of medicine, and a long list of emergency phone numbers. My grandfather had just spent the last four months struggling for his life in a hospital room, and the effects of pneumonia, heart failure, and septic shock had transformed him into a person I barely recognized. As he entered our home, I stood back and watched his heroic efforts to take a small step and I listened to his humble attempts to utter a simple word. I was overwhelmed with sorrow and hopelessness.

Over the next few weeks, I watched and waited for improvement. I saw none. Instead, I saw my grandfather unable to shower, shave, or dress himself without help from my father or uncles. I saw my grandfather unable to remember what he had eaten, unable to remember my name, and unable to remember when to take his medicines. I kept looking for the grandfather I had once known, but found only a weak, fragile, and confused person. Somewhere between all his therapy appointments and trips to the emergency room, I gave up hope that my grandfather would ever return to me. Gradually, it became much easier for me to isolate myself, to totally immerse myself in homework or flute practice rather than face my grandfather.

But then I read *Two Old Women,* and in Ch'idzigyaak and Sa', I found the hope and the strength I needed to look at my grandfather and help him make his journey. As I discovered Ch'idzigyaak's and Sa's perseverance and determination to survive, I began to regain a sense of hope and possibility when I watched my grandfather's efforts that I had once considered pointless. I began to respect and admire his determination to remove his own socks at night, to take small steps on his own, to dress himself. I understood that my grandfather, like Ch'idzigyaak and Sa', wanted to hold his "chin up proudly" just as they had held theirs up when they were abandoned by their tribe and were struggling for survival.

As I read *Two Old Women,* I realized that, like the tribe that had abandoned Ch'idzigyaak and Sa' because they had only seen "two weak old women," I had only seen a weak old man and had abandoned my grandfather. With this realization, I then began to look at my grandfather differently and I began to understand life from his perspective. I felt his humiliation, his frustration, and his wounded pride. When Ch'idzigyaak and Sa' made the decision "Let us die trying," I understood why my grandfather would rather take ten minutes to walk down a hallway than be pushed in a wheelchair. Instead of seeing a stubborn old man when

I looked at my grandfather, I saw resilience, determination, and courage.

As I got to know Ch'idzigyaak and Sa', I began to wonder if my grandfather, like Ch'idzigyaak and Sa', felt as though he were "condemned to die" and everyone had given up on him. But Sa' and Ch'idzigyaak had given me courage to conquer my fears, and now, instead of avoiding my grandfather, I began to spend more time with him. Instead of practicing flute with a closed bedroom door, I played music for him to enjoy and watched him smile as his body and mind found relaxation. Instead of reading alone in my bedroom, I began to sit next to my grandfather and read his favorite books to him. I learned to listen long enough to let him speak, and I listened long enough to hear stories of his childhood and see him gain strength from those memories. I was no longer afraid of his suffering, and I learned to touch him again, to hug him, and to soothe his loneliness and fear. I also learned to accept his limitations and love him regardless of those limitations.

Thank you, Ms. Wallis, for writing *Two Old Women* and sharing the legend of Ch'idzigyaak and Sa' with me, because without those two incredibly strong women, I would still be inside the walls of my own world, trying to escape the suffering of my grandfather. Instead, with these two women, I have been able to face my own fears, make my own journey, and discover in my grandfather a person of incredible resilience and inner strength.

Anna Marie Wichorek

The Kite Runner
KHALED HOSSEINI

"I became lost in the Kabul of Amir's childhood."
Audrey [last name withheld by request]

As a child growing up in Afghanistan, Khaled Hosseini loved reading and especially writing. "I was probably eight or nine years old when I began writing," he says. "I was really passionate about it. I felt so in my element when I was writing."

Hosseini did not pursue writing as a career, at least not at first. He became a doctor. But his passion for writing could not be denied, and in 2001, he began writing *The Kite Runner*, a story based on his childhood in Kabul, Afghanistan. Then, after the terrorist attacks on America in September of that same year, the doctor considered putting away his pen. Suddenly, Muslims — all Muslims — were potential terrorists. His wife urged him to keep writing.

The Kite Runner is not a memoir. Still, there are autobiographical connections between the author and his character Amir. They both love reading and literature, watching American western movies from the 1960s and 1970s, and they especially enjoy kite fighting. They share, too, the experiences of growing up in wealthy neighbor-hoods of Kabul. But while fictional Amir's family was there in 1980, when the Soviet Union invaded Afghanistan, the Hosseini family was living in Paris. Unable to return to their native home, the family sought asylum in the United States. Like the author, Amir eventually found himself in America struggling to make a new life. This not uncommon story of Middle Easterners immigrating to America had not been widely told before.

Dear Mr. Hosseini,

Iowa is *not* flat. I can't remember how many times I was told this. When my family migrated to Iowa from Washington, D.C., nine years ago, friends jokingly reminded us to trade in our car for a tractor. A classmate told me that people in Iowa didn't have pets — they had pigs. My second-grade teacher even rolled out the map and pointed at Iowa with her yardstick. "This is Iowa," she said authoritatively. "It is the number one producer of corn in the nation."

True, Iowa has its cornfields, pig farms, and John Deeres, but these stereotypes don't determine what Iowa is all about. The people here are diverse, well traveled, and urbane; they don't fit the images portrayed by "Iowa jokes." Once I realized that none of the stereotypes about Iowa were true, I became wary of other falsehoods as well. I thought I could sight stereotypes like a big-game hunter, but it turns out I was wrong.

Since September 11, 2001, America's perception of the Middle East has changed for the worse. When young people today hear the word "Afghanistan," certain images may come to mind: the Taliban, Osama bin Laden, veiled women, Muslim extremists. The list goes on. I'll admit I felt embarrassed once I began your novel *The Kite Runner* and realized that I was guilty of holding stereotypes as well. The majority of my knowledge of the Middle East had come from Michael Moore and *Aladdin*, two sources that failed me by chapter 2. The more I read about the Afghanistan of Amir's past and present, the more I realized it was I who had been veiled all along.

Your novel tantalized my senses. I could almost smell the kabob at the bazaar, hear the haggling voices in the Afghan flea market, and feel the slice of Amir's kite string against my fingers. This rendition of Afghanistan, much richer than anything proliferated by the American media, is what swept me into your book. I became lost in the Kabul of Amir's childhood.

Even after finishing your novel, my fascination with Afghan culture didn't fade. Other books were forgotten in the dusty recesses of my mind, but yours demanded my attention. The agonizingly beautiful description of pre- and post-Taliban Afghanistan enticed me. I was heartbroken to see the Afghanistan of the 1970s lose its flavor as the Taliban drove in with their tanks and pickup trucks.

Your portrayal of Afghanistan as a battleground for the United States, Russia, and the Taliban further changed my view of Afghanistan. I no longer view it along stereotypical lines and have begun to associate this country with its population and culture, not the actions of a select few.

My epiphany only fascinated me further. I rifled through the shelves of my library, looking for nonfiction books about the Middle East. I nosed through geographical atlases, sneezing on the musty pages. I finally struck gold while browsing through the brochures by the library entrance. One struck me in particular: it was an advertisement for a summer institute on Middle Eastern culture. Within a week I had sent out an application. A few months later, I was accepted.

Mr. Hosseini, if it hadn't been for your novel, I would not be where I am today. Your book was eye-opening, to use a cliché with all possible seriousness, and it awoke me to other opportunities. At the summer institute, I was able to visit a mosque, examine artifacts, pluck at instruments, and sample foods from the other side of the world. I would never have attempted to do any of these things had your novel not haunted me for months after turning the last page.

It took a second reading of your book for me to grasp its magnitude and relevance. Our world is a changing place; the vicissitudes of life will outpace us if we do not strive to understand other countries and cultures before it is too late. Amir turned his back on Hassan, but we cannot allow ourselves to do the same to other nations. I have become motivated to learn about other countries whose fates are inextricably tied to ours. Someday, I would like to be the one who can encourage nations to set aside their differences and, in the words of Rahim Khan, find "a way to be good again."

I am inspired, Mr. Hosseini, by this expanded world view that pulls me further than the borders of my state. I think it is fitting to express my gratitude using some words from Hassan: Thank you "a thousand times over."

Audrey

She's Come Undone
WALLY LAMB

"I no longer hide in my flannel sheets, waiting
for my problems to disappear."
Gabrielle Sclafani

"I don't love to write, but I love figuring out what's going to happen to these characters I worry about," says Wally Lamb. "I feel parental toward them, and I worry that they'll come out okay. Some of my best days are when they surprise me." Lamb's character Dolores Price, the protagonist of his novel *She's Come Undone*, surprised him. Despite physical and mental abuse she suffered as an adolescent and young adult, Dolores is a survivor who finds love and self-contentment. Lamb based his character, in part, on his memory of a former student who had sat scowling in the back of his English classroom. Like Dolores, this student was overweight. Also like Dolores, she was ignored by others and obviously unhappy. His attempts as a teacher to draw her out failed. But in writing *She's Come Undone*, the author imagined her pain and in doing so, touched the lives of many other young people.

Dear Wally Lamb,

Its intriguing blue cover dusted with acclamations, your novel *She's Come Undone* sat on my bookshelf for several months before I dared to pick it up. It wasn't that I thought it would be uninteresting or that I was swamped with other books to read. Rather, I'd heard too many times that it was depressing and deep —"heavy reading." I'd been struggling with a serious autoimmune disorder, Wegener's granulomatosis, for over two years. I was, and still am, on corticosteroids and a mild chemotherapy medication. I didn't want a depressing book; I wanted one that would lift my spirits, something funny that didn't require too much thought. And quite honestly, there was something about the girl's face on the cover, peeking out from behind a mask of clouds, that struck a chord in me which I wasn't sure I wanted struck. Yet the book kept tempting and teasing me, not satisfied to be neglected, and the day my fingers finally wrapped themselves around its silky spine, I began an unbreakable connection.

Despite my reservations, your words engulfed me from the moment I began reading, as the waves of the Atlantic often did when I was younger. It was scary, I'll admit, but simultaneously wonderful and exhilarating. As your novel focuses on Dolores's painful journey through adolescence and into adulthood, it paints a stark picture of the brutality and prejudices of the real world. Reading about her struggles against herself and the humanity, or lack thereof, around her provided me with a telescopic view inside my own mind. After reading how Dolores deals with her rape, I saw that it wasn't all that different from the way I reacted to my diagnosis. We both chose to hide from our circumstances and isolate ourselves from our loved ones. We felt, ultimately, that we had lost control. Dolores's body may have been raped by a man, but I, too, was raped in a sense, at the hands of nature and modern medicine.

When he prescribed the steroids, my doctor didn't even look at me. Though I can never get inside his mind, I have a decent idea as to why. He was ashamed. He knew — as Jack did when he took advantage of Dolores — that my body would never again be my own. The steroids caused my face to swell and break out in an acne-like rash to the point where people who didn't see me every day often didn't recognize me when they did. The drugs played with my mind so much that I could rarely think straight. The only solace I found from the constant churning of anxieties through my mind were the few cherished hours of sleep I stole each evening. During the day, however, my life was a living hell. I had trouble turning my jumbled thoughts into sentences, and every time I tried to communicate, a flurry of stuttered phrases fell out of my mouth. Even with a daily regimen of antidepressants, there were many times when suicide was more than a fleeting image across my radar screen. Knowing that this lay in store for me, my doctor probably wanted to dissociate himself as much as possible from me. To him, I was just another name — a check from the insurance company, just like, to Jack, Dolores is just some girl who gave him a few minutes of pleasure.

But the blame I put on my doctor was ultimately a way for me to give my enemy a face — my true bête noire was my disease. It was easy for us to turn our hatred for our assailants into a hatred for ourselves, because it provided an outlet for the brutality we wished we could inflict on them. They got to escape, but we live with the memories of our pain each and every day. They made us feel worthless and powerless, to the point where we truly despised ourselves. In the same way that the cells inside my body were attacking each other, my mind quickly became my own worst enemy. What's the point of fighting, I thought, when there's no guarantee, when the end result might not even be an improvement?

When Dolores attempts to drown herself, she scared me. *Is this my fate?* I asked myself. Furtively, I flipped through the pages and lived each word, feeling the chill of the ocean against our skin, thinned by the stretch marks we both know too well. I could see our hands, translucent shells bobbing with the waves. And when Dolores finds the courage not to give up, to wade back to shore, she pulls me in, too, with her magnetic charge of empathy. I drew myself back to reality, and took a huge gasp, suddenly realizing that I'd been holding my breath as the events unfurled between the pages. And I've known, since that instant, that if Dolores can make it, then so can I. We've already *been* through hell; we can't give up now. Yes, we have battle wounds, but they don't stop us from being vivacious, compelling, and undeniably strong.

I'm proud to say that since reading your book, I no longer hide in my flannel sheets, waiting for my problems to disappear. I've become proactive. I go to the gym, baby-sit, and do my homework. I've rediscovered hobbies I thought I had lost interest in such as gardening and writing. One of my biggest challenges — one that Dolores also faced — has been reengaging with people and making friends. Like Dolores, I have managed to develop new bonds with positive people who make me feel good about myself, as opposed to trying — with futility — to meet the standards of critical or demanding friends, a lesson both Dolores and I learned the hard way. And most important, I am learning, little by little, to love myself.

Thank you, Mr. Lamb. You have taught me, through Dolores and her painfully empowering journey, the importance of knowing my own value. Dolores finds her beauty through layers of degradation and self-mutilation; I know I can find mine, too.

Sincerely,
Gabrielle Sclafani

The Wall and the Wing
LAURA RUBY

"I was weighed down, coated in a layer of plastic."
Emily Waller

"I come from a family that changed drastically through divorce and abandonment," Laura Ruby says. "Whether I like it or not, I've been shaped by those events but I hope I'm not doomed by them." Writing is one way that Ruby deals with her feelings from her childhood constructively, and family relationships are often at the heart of the books she writes. In *The Wall and the Wing*, Gurl and Bug conspire to escape Hope House for the Homeless and Hopeless in a New York City where some people can fly and some can be invisible.

Dear Laura Ruby,

A curious question can lead to answers that are deeper than anyone might realize. "Would you rather have the power of invisibility or the power to fly?" This question inspired your novel *The Wall and the Wing*, but it also inspired me. Instantly I know what my original answer would have been. I would have wanted nothing more than

to slip through the cracks in the world and slink, unde-
tected, away from prying eyes (or really, any eyes at all).
While it's true that I am a little afraid of heights, there's
something I used to fear even more: judgment.

In your book, those who don't have the ability to fly
are labeled as leadfeet, social outcasts who are quite literally weighed down to earth while watching everybody else
soar high above them. I was remarkably similar to a leadfoot when, in seventh grade, I was diagnosed with a spinal
disease called kyphosis. While it didn't pose any serious
medical threat, I was forced to wear a back brace — a big
honking piece of outlandish plastic that encased me like a
shell. While it was keeping me from being a hunchback,
that brace may as well have weighed a million pounds. I
went from trying on outfit after outfit, wearing different
dresses and skirts, to only wearing baggy sweatpants and
extra-large T-shirts because that was the only thing that
would conceal my brace. Not only was there the physical discomfort of the brace, but I became horrendously
self-conscious, a turtle who always retreats inside its shell.
But the absolute worst thing of all about my brace was
being in the presence of other kids at school. I watched
all my friends have great new experiences and create long-
lasting friendships, becoming popular and even beginning
to date. From my own perspective, it felt as if I were standing miles below a cloudless blue sky, watching the people
who I longed to be with soar above me. While I still

laughed and smiled with them, pretending to be enjoying myself, there was always a nagging part of me, reminding me that we weren't the same. I was weighed down, coated in a layer of plastic. They were free.

As I continued reading, getting to know Gurl and Bug, I really felt as if they were my friends, because I could relate to their emotions of feeling useless and isolated. As Gurl develops her invisibility and Bug has his odd adventures, I felt motivated to do something to change myself. Unfortunately, I lacked the skill to spontaneously develop superpowers, so I did the next best thing and started making friends. While I was too shy to speak to the more popular kids in my class, I approached those who, like me, were more socially outcast. Not only did I make friends, but I also started to stop feeling so sorry for myself.

When I finally closed your book, something strange occurred. I realized that while I had been inside the pages, I hadn't focused on how I looked or what others thought of me with my brace on. I had been so immersed, enjoying myself with the characters, that it simply hadn't mattered. That realization led me to another. It wasn't the other people around me who had made me feel like a leadfoot. I had excluded and isolated myself, feeling worthless, although my friends were perfectly accepting of my brace. I missed out on opportunities and maybe I couldn't wear the clothes I wanted, but that didn't have to keep me from having fun and making great new friends. At first I'd been hostile to my old friends and hadn't accepted any new ones because I was worried that I would fail, when I hadn't even tried in the first place.

My perspective shifted violently after reading this book, and while it's true that there were other factors that made me realize that I was the one weighing myself down, reading about the characters' experiences showed me that if you have a goal, you should always strive for it, no matter how impossible. Differences are never negative — diversity is what makes the world worth living in. While my situation wasn't positive, I could still make the best out of my middle-school years. Our own experiences shape our lives, whether they are positive or negative, and it doesn't matter if you're wearing a huge plastic back brace or not as long as you're having a good time and learning a little about life. What matters is that you live, learn, and love as much of life as you can, and your book helped me to understand that truth. "Would you rather have the power of invisibility or the power to fly?" My answer is still the same as before. I would choose invisibility, but not for the same reasons. I would choose invisibility so I could sneak more chocolate-chip cookies without getting caught.

Emily Waller

"Sonnet LXVI"
PABLO NERUDA

"It is difficult to reconcile my hate and my love."
Hannah DesChamp

"My duty was to serve the Chilean people in my actions and with my poetry," said Pablo Neruda. "I have lived singing and defending them."

As a teenager, Neftali Ricardo Reyes Basoalto wrote poetry despite his father, who felt the literary life would be unprofitable or worse — corrupting. But the young man followed his heart. He eventually changed his name to Pablo Neruda and continued to write, becoming well known throughout Chile and the world for his poems.

Neruda's fame drew him into politics, and he traveled as a consul to various countries throughout the world. His politics were progressive, favoring the rights of the people and the poor. In 1970, he was nominated as a candidate for president, but he ultimately declined the nomination. His primary duty, he said, was to the Chilean people, singing their stories, celebrating their spirit, and defending their rights.

Dear Pablo Neruda,

As kids, everyone has confused feelings toward their family. My feelings toward my family are complicated and sometimes terrible. I have always felt isolated and guilty about my relationship with my mom and dad, until I came across your poem "Sonnet LXVI," with the line "I don't love you only because I love you."

My dad turned his back on my mother, my brother, and me when I was six years old. He betrayed us and lied, and never returned. My mother was forced to raise two children at the age of twenty-two with no support. The pressure was too much for her, and two years later she had to go to drug rehabilitation. My brother and I moved in with my best friend and her family for three months as my mother tried to get clean.

While in rehabilitation, my mom met someone and decided to leave with him. My brother and I moved back in with her, Jason (her new boyfriend), and his two sons. After only a couple of months, my mom was pregnant. Jason proposed to her, and they got married. Shortly after the wedding, my little sister, Nevaeh Rain, was born.

Five months after Nevaeh's birth, Jason disappeared, leaving us on the streets again. My mom knew someone we could rent a room from, except there were a few problems. All four of us had to share a tiny room and all sleep on one queen-size bed. Every morning to get to school, we had to take two buses and walk. It was difficult, and things could've been better, but my mom loved us just as much as any other mom loves her children and she was trying to make life work for all of us.

About a week before Halloween when I was in fifth grade, my mom did not pick me up after school. I called her, my uncle, my grandparents; nobody answered. Finally, at eight o'clock, the administrator at the school let my friend's mom take me home. She took me to get dinner and then took me to my house. As I walked in the door to my house, I did not see anyone. I went to my room to find my seven-year-old brother sitting on the bed holding my little sister. I asked where Mom was, and he did not respond. I called my friend's mom, crying, begging her to pick me up. She refused, telling me I could not abandon my siblings, as my mom had done. So I dried my tears and took care of my little sister and brother.

There was no response from my mom for three years. By that time, I was living with my godmother and her husband with my little brother. My sister was living with her father, and I wasn't able to see her for two years.

I don't really know why my dad left. I guess the thought of supporting a family was scary to him, and he had his own problems that he had to deal with. My mom has apologized and explained herself, but it is difficult to reconcile my hate and my love for her as a person and her actions.

She had her problems; she didn't have any money and had no friends to borrow money from. She was thirsty, thirsty for the thrill that being careless held, so she went to the bar and drank away her problems. I don't really know what she did for those missing years. Maybe she made up for the high-school years she missed because of me. I now know that she had to leave us, but she just didn't have the strength to tell us that. My mom was and is a caring and loving person. All she wanted was to love and be loved in return. So now I have forgiven her and what she did to my siblings and me.

When I came across your poem, the first people I thought of were my mom and my dad. I don't love them, except for the utter reason that I love them. They are my parents; they are the reason I am here and the reason I am who I am. I have to love them, even after what they've put me through. But because of what they have done to my brother, my sister, and me, a part of me despises them. This is why when I read "I hate you endlessly, and in hating you I beg you, / and it's the measure of my vagrant love / not to see you and yet to love you blindly too," I was infatuated. My love for my parents changes every time their names tumble through my mind.

"Not to see you and yet to love you blindly." I do not see my parents, and I don't really know who they are. I love them without knowing them, and I didn't think that was possible until I read this line. This gave me hope. Hope that maybe I'm not crazy, and that it's okay to feel this way. Your poem gave me the explanation I've been searching for — the reason why and the reason how we can love without loving and hate without hating.

Hannah DesChamp

The Things They Carried
TIM O'BRIEN

"Words seemed weak and cruelly useless."
Alexandra McLaughlin

"I was a coward. I went to war," Tim O'Brien has said. In the summer of 1968, O'Brien received two documents: his college diploma and his draft notice. Throughout college, he had protested the involvement of American troops in Vietnam. If he reported to the draft board, as his notice required him to, he would become one of those troops, senselessly entangled in another country's civil war. Or he could dodge the draft by running away to Canada.

He thought about his dilemma all that summer. Day after day he debated. His father had served as a sailor in World War II. His mother, too, had served in that war, as a WAVE. What would be the emotional consequences both for himself and for them if he ran? In search of clarity and tempted to run, he spent time fishing on the Rainy River near the Canadian border. O'Brien has told this story many times, and he always ends it with a postscript: It isn't true. It didn't happen that way. He never went fishing on the Rainy River with the intention of dodging the draft. But in another sense, he explains, it is true because it was what he was thinking and feeling at the time. By imagining the story, he made it real.

"On the Rainy River" is the fourth story in *The Things They Carried*, his story collection about soldiers serving in Vietnam. But "war stories aren't always about war . . . bombs and bullets . . . tactics . . . foxholes and canteen," he has said. "War stories, like any good story, are finally about the human heart." And young readers know that. O'Brien's younger readers relate his book to their own personal experiences, not war but rather "a bad childhood or a broken home," he says. "And these are the things they're carrying."

Dear Tim O'Brien,

A twelve-dollar digital watch from Target. A bottle of ibuprofen. A heart-shaped gold ring my mom wore when she was a teenager. Vanilla-scented hand lotion. The memory of my mom lying lifeless and still on a hospital bed, her cold hands no longer squeezing back. A shoe box containing a lifetime of letters, some creased, worn, and stained with tears. My sister's sleepy but comforting voice through the phone at two a.m., when I lie awake, haunted by the past and crippled by fears: "I know. It will be okay. I love you."

These are the things I carry.

Two years ago, when I was a sophomore in high school, my mom had a sudden heart attack while running. She collapsed on the side of the road. My English class read *The Things They Carried* a few months later. What I expected was just another book about war. What I found was a message that spoke directly to my soul. Your book came when I felt my suburban town was the quintessential land of lollipops and ignorance, when I feared that real pain and heartache were foreign to everyone but me. It came when I needed it the most.

I've wanted to become a writer ever since I could remember. Yet after the death of my mom, words seemed weak and cruelly useless. After all, a world where my mom could have a physical and be characterized as the "picture of perfect health" and then die a week later was not a world in which words were valuable. Writing could not change the past. Writing could not change anything. That was what I thought until I read your book.

I was not even alive during the Vietnam War, yet you brought me to that place. Through Rat Kiley's torture of the baby water buffalo, you stunned me with a gruesome physical image of emotional grief. If you could help me understand a war fought halfway across the world three decades before I was born, maybe I, too, could reach others with my words.

You tell a story about Norman Bowker returning from war. He overflows with terrible memories and stories, yet he has no one to tell. His father never asks. His neighbors never ask. No one ever asks. This is how I felt after my mom died. My naive and trusting demeanor shattered; I could no longer view the world the same way. I was annoyed, even angry, at the unchanged dynamics at school and with my friends. My life had just been ripped apart, and in those first intense months of grief, it seemed as though no one even noticed.

Worst of all, no one asked about my mom. People were so afraid of saying something wrong that they closed their mouths and kept them that way. It was as if my mom — who woke up every morning to run because it made her feel alive, who spent hours in her garden, who sang in the kitchen as she washed dishes, who loved her children so much she lay awake at night worrying about us — had never existed.

I could not understand this, but I was being forced to accept it. When the soldier eventually kills himself, I was jolted awake. Why are death, war, and loss such taboo subjects? Why must we bury them down deep inside, cover our fears and uncertainties with a strained smile, and ignore a whole part of ourselves? No longer was I going to hide the past and the pain. I wouldn't give up because people were unwilling to listen. I would spin words into poetry and attempt to define the indefinable. Circumstances had broken my heart, weighed down my shoulders, and given me a lifelong burden to carry. Yet I was unwilling to succumb to the same fate as the disillusioned soldier. I would not be shattered.

Your last story simultaneously opened fresh wounds and gave me the first real comfort since my mom's death. I cried when Linda died. It was tragic. She was so young. I thought of my mom and it was almost unbearable. However, I realized from your book that stories could keep a person alive. Stories allow us to visit the past how it was: untainted in its beauty and unmarked by death or struggle.

Thank you for telling these stories, Mr. O'Brien. Thank you for the painfully honest and emotional descriptions of war. Thank you for giving me comfort and hope in a time that was clouded by darkness and uncertainty. Your poignant words in *The Things They Carried* will forever be included in the things I carry. You helped me see that I am not alone.

Alexandra McLaughlin

"If"

RUDYARD KIPLING

> "My mother was my salvation from my father."
> Joshua Tiprigan

"Words are, of course, the most powerful drug used by mankind," Rudyard Kipling once said. Words were indeed powerful for the British author. He earned his living working with words, first as a journalist and later as a poet and novelist. In 1907, he received the Nobel Prize in Literature. Among his works are the novels *The Jungle Book* and *Kim* and poems such as "Gunga Din" and "If."

Rudyard Kipling wrote "If" as a tribute to a friend and military officer who had faced defeat in battle. The poem came to represent stoicism, the British tradition of maintaining "a stiff upper lip" in times of adversity. It is written in the form of advice from a father to a son, and this framework took on a deeper poignancy when Kipling's only son was reported missing in France during World War I. Kipling was also in France, working as a war correspondent. He searched army field hospitals, hoping to find his son or learn that he had been taken prisoner. His search was futile. Although a body was never found, Lieutenant John Kipling was declared dead.

Dear Rudyard Kipling,

My dad is a six-foot-tall, deep-voiced, husky eastern European rock of a man. In fact, all the men on my dad's side of the family are a bunch of Romanian macho hunks with bulging biceps and visages as stony and solemn as statues. Genetically, I have these same features, yet, because of my mother's influence, I am much softer on the inside. Instead of wrestling or boxing at family gatherings, like my cousins so often do, I would much rather read a book or talk to my older relatives. Although to my father I seem quiet, unaggressive, or altogether "unmanly," he has consistently tried to instill a sense of being a man in me ever since I was very young. When I reached the age of twelve, he began taking me to his auto-body shop, which he built up from nothing as an immigrant entrepreneur. He told me this tough job would build me into a man of character. I would work grueling hours sanding cars and preparing them for paint. My dad also urges me to lift weights to make me strong like a man. My perception of being a man has mostly been molded by how my rugged dad portrays himself. But this all changed a year ago when my mother passed away and I stumbled upon your poem "If."

My mother was my salvation from my father and was the one person who could understand me. If I ever got tired during my work hours at the shop, I could call her to come and pick me up and she would do the impossible, reason with my father. It was my mother who instilled the love of literature and languages in me. My mother spoke six languages fluently and had thousands of books, which still sit in the attic of our house. A couple of months after my mother's death, I wandered up the cold creaky stairs that lead into the attic, shuffled through some books, and found a large one that was filled with poetry. In this book, I found "If." As I read the poem, the words printed in black ink seemed to turn to golden truths and values that burned deep into my brain and trickled down to my heart, gently caressing some wet droplets to my eyes, but I was not "man" enough to cry, so I quickly blinked them away.

Ever since the death of my mother, I have felt alone, as if I belong to no family. The image of a man that I saw in my dad was completely shattered when I saw him break down and cry, which looked so pathetic and "unmanly" compared to his usual stoic and emotionless countenance. My grandmother blamed my father and me for causing the cancer that took my mother away in less than a month's time after the doctor's diagnosis. In return, the blame was doubled upon my shoulders as my dad turned on me and started shouting more about things that don't matter, yet I remained silent, remembering the golden words: "If you can keep your head when all about you / Are losing theirs and blaming it on you . . . you'll be a Man, my son."

"If" reminded me to remain calm and "keep my head" because I wanted to be a man and wanted to be the one supporting my family. Throughout the struggles that quickly took over my life as well as my father's, I remained strong while he seemed to crumble and fold under the pressure. Since my mother was a stay-at-home mom, I sacrificed my ability to compete in a winter sport so that I could stay home and cook for my family and clean the house in order to try to take up the jobs that my mother was not around to do. My father saw this, and our relationship has grown much stronger. He finally respects me for who I am and has told me that he is proud to have a man for his son. Through this poem, I realized that to be a man is not about putting weights on a barbell but rather putting the weight of others on your back.

Your poem was so much more than just a simple list of guidelines or morals that some see it as; it really changed my life and my relationship with my dad. Because of "If," I am able to walk with my chest pushed out like a man, not because of bulging pectoral muscles but because of the heart under them.

With admiration and thanks,

Joshua Tiprigan

Does My Head Look Big in This?
RANDA ABDEL-FATTAH

"The judgmental, racist, hateful monster
I feared was myself."
Xiomara Torres

"It became apparent to me that the only time Muslim females appeared as heroines in books were as escapees of the Taliban, victims of an honour killing, or subjects of the Saudi royalty!" Randa Abdel-Fattah once bemoaned. As a Muslim woman who is both a writer and a lawyer, she is very much aware of gender and racial stereotypes expressed in politics and popular culture. And so she created Amal, a sixteen-year-old girl who decides to become a "full-timer" and wear a hijab, or head scarf. *Does My Head Look Big in This?* is Amal's story. She's not forced to wear the hijab by a man but makes the decision to embrace her faith as part of her gender identity even in the face of taunts and racial discrimination.

Ms. Randa Abdel-Fattah,

Last summer I read your book *Does My Head Look Big in This?* I can't be sure, but I think it was a Saturday afternoon. I remember being encircled by a plethora of snacks that I had abducted from the kitchen cabinets, swathed in a cocoon I had created out of my Harry Potter fleece blanket. I sat down that day anticipating all the cliché elements of a YA fiction: first, the ever-popular cafeteria scene, followed by the introduction of the various cliques; next, the heroine's first kiss with the dreamy boy she has stalked since third grade but never really thought she had a chance with; the big misunderstanding that loses her a friend; and finally, the cheerily fake conclusion of it all where everyone goes home happy.

What I expected was your standard, stereotypical teen novel; a watered-down Gossip Girl book. What I got was a wake-up call. Amal Abdel-Hakim was my wake-up call. Amal was that little voice in the back of my head that I had battled my whole life. Amal was me: a teenage girl trying to survive in a racially imbalanced world while striving to hold on to her identity. Amal was me, with one exception: I had been trying to forget.

A year ago, if you had asked me about my race, I would have begrudgingly admitted that I was Puerto Rican and then swiftly changed the subject. The truth is, I was ashamed of my nationality. I did not want to be Hispanic. I resented the fact that I had been born into my big Latino family, so I attempted to conceal it. I did everything in my power to separate myself from the stereotypes about the Puerto Rican race. I paraded my obsession with rock music and my obviously punk style in clothing. I made sure everyone knew that my best friend was white and that I thought shaggy-haired skaters were adorable. I straightened my overabundance of tightly curled hair whenever I had the chance. Instead of Xiomara or even my usual nickname, Xio, I demanded that everyone call me Mara because it sounded more at home among the mass of Rachels, Alis, and Courtneys at my high school. And my unbreakable golden rule: NEVER EVER SPEAK SPANISH. EVER.

I was embarrassed by myself and by so many aspects of my life. I hated my small, poor inner-city school because it swarmed with Puerto Ricans, Mexicans, and Cubans like myself. I constantly and publicly put down "ghetto" kids in hopes of deflecting any notions that I myself was one. Reggaeton, rap, hip-hop and salsa were, to me, nonexistent genres of music. Although I never bragged, I prided myself on the fact that I was number one in my class because I felt that it somehow made up for my "sin" of being Hispanic. When I was nagged once about learning to speak Spanish, I remember yelling, "We are in America! Before Spanish even crosses our minds, we should learn to speak proper English!" I was always paranoid that behind my back, someone would be judging me, stereotyping me, making jokes about me, counting me out because of my race.

What I never realized was that the judgmental, racist, hateful monster I feared was myself.

Your character Amal helped me to see that. When I finished your book, I realized that my entire life had been consumed by an endless, unwinnable race that I had created. I was running from myself, from something I could never stop. I realized that my actions and attitude toward myself and toward my people as well as my entire outlook on life had been hypocritical, wrong, and ignorant. I realized who I was. I acknowledged the fact that I am and always will be intrinsically, unavoidably, undeniably, and wonderfully Hispanic. Spanish courses through my veins, and I had been blocking its path, cutting off my blood supply, slowly killing who I was.

I am Puerto Rican, and I can say that now easily, contentedly, even proudly, thanks to you and your book. Just as Amal made the decision to wear the hijab in public full-time, I now also don my own hijab of sorts. I have decided to embrace my heritage and allow it to flower inside of me as well as manifest itself on the outside, for everyone to see. I have learned, with the help of your book, that my race does not define who I am but that it will always be a part of me. To become who I truly want to be, I have to embrace who I already am: a tan-skinned, curly-haired, rock-music-loving, SPANISH-SPEAKING *puertorriqueña*. Thank you for the wake-up call.

Yours,

Xiomara Torres

The Joy Luck Club
AMY TAN

"My mother sits at her corner in the East,
and I at the West."
Ayesha Usmani

Amy Tan received her first writing award when she was eight years old and in the third grade. "What the Library Means to Me" was a short essay she entered in a local contest. She wrote about giving her "entire life savings," which happened to be just seventeen cents, to the Citizens for Santa Rosa Library and she urged others to do the same. The author smiles remembering that first award and says, "There was a little gleam in my mind that maybe writing could be lucrative."

That early success, however, did not impress her mother to the point where she encouraged Amy to keep writing. Rather, her mother forced her to practice piano and study hard to become a doctor. In her mother's eyes, medicine was the better career choice. But Tan was rebellious and followed her own path, pursuing her love of art and writing. She hadn't thought of becoming a writer of fiction until her business partner told her that she'd never "make a dime" writing on her own. Tan decided that she could either believe him or prove him wrong.

Dear Amy Tan,

My mother sits at her corner at the table: the East, her home, her memories. I sit at the West, opposite from her. East and West, two cultures constantly colliding, but both fitting in one world. Fitting together like mah-jongg tiles, but I cannot see. I see our definite differences. I see the distance between us. I see her coming toward me, but I run away, far away to the other side of the world. I love the West, but must I give up the East?

The sun rises in the East and kisses the sky with its golden hues, and my mother rises and pounds the dough with her small, flour-covered hands. A new idea dawns in her head as she twists and stretches the dough. She calls me, and I grudgingly come downstairs, groggy and confused because it's seven in the morning. My mother has that gleam in her eyes. I have seen that look before — a look that makes you cringe and twist in annoyance and despair. I reluctantly snatch the dough from the plate and start rolling and pounding it. Smack, thud, and flip. By the end of the cooking lesson, I am covered in flour, the trash can is overflowing with my disasters, and my mother is frustrated. I wash my face with a splash of cold water and look up. Your character June stares at me from the mirror. She whispers about not letting my mother change and control me.

My mother wanders about the store, and I make sure I wander in another direction. I come with her to the checkout line, avoiding the peculiar stares of the salesclerk.

My mother asks, in her not-so-perfect English, if there is a sale. The clerk mumbles an answer, and my mother is confused. I quietly whisper to her in Urdu that the sale was last week. My mother responds to me loudly in Urdu, and I feel embarrassed. I distance myself from her as we head toward the car. People turn and look at us, muffling their giggles. I am imagining, but I am not imagining, the shame. Why doesn't my mother understand me? Can't she fit in with American culture? Your character Waverly shines within me. Independent, stubborn, and ashamed of cultural ties, I mimic her moves and prepare for the attack.

I must transcend these linguistic and cultural barriers. Barriers that block me from my mother. A mother, with all her energy, who loves and guides me. This guidance must direct me to a new path — a path that will allow me to appreciate my mother and my vibrant culture.

I wear my *shalwar kameez* and brush my hair back. I feel uncomfortable. I carefully pour green tea for my aunt and uncles. I feel subservient. I sit upright and talk, mostly listen, with my grandmother. I feel bored. I listen quietly and patiently to my mother and aunts complain about prices, daughters, cooking, husbands, aging, and daughters. I feel awkward. I look aimlessly out the window, and your character Jing-mei stares back at me.

I strive to find the connection with my mother — a connection that will balance independence and loyalty to my heritage. A balance of Pakistani values of love, obedience, and humility in harmony with American values of independence, free speech, and self-esteem. A journey that will always be difficult but worth the effort. I have come to desire that connection through your guidance, Amy Tan. A connection that I have now found. My mother sits at her corner in the East, and I at the West. But we unite in harmony. A harmony that appreciates our similarities and our dependence on each other.

With sincere gratitude,
Ayesha Usmani

The Joy Luck Club
AMY TAN

"I, too, take advantage of my mother."
Lisa Le

In 1987, Amy Tan traveled with her mother to visit relatives in China. Tan had often been resentful of her mother when she was a teenager, but on this trip, she saw a very different woman. That was Tan's "turning point," she says, and adds, "I couldn't have written *The Joy Luck Club* without having been there, without having felt that spiritual sense of geography." Amy Tan had found her past in China and in doing so, found her writer's voice.

Dear Amy Tan,

Before reading your novel *The Joy Luck Club*, I saw my mother as someone I couldn't connect to and didn't want to relate to. When looking back, I feel ashamed of myself. I remember doing nothing while my mother and I drifted further apart. When I was in sixth grade, your novel gave me insight about the value of family and the differences in cultures between generations. I've realized that miscommunication and a language barrier drove me and my mother apart, and as time progressed, that gap widened.

My mother left Vietnam to come to the United States in 1997 while she was pregnant with me. She still hasn't assimilated to American culture and even now in 2014 struggles with speaking and learning English. At home she used to speak to me in Vietnamese and I would answer in English. It's not that I couldn't speak Vietnamese — I understood the basics — it was because I didn't want to. I never took the time to appreciate my mother and to consider her feelings about my behavior and the alienation she felt toward American culture. She grew up in southern Vietnam, learning traditional customs, whereas I grew up in D.C. with an entirely different set of beliefs and experiences. I remember always being confused whenever she used common Vietnamese proverbs to give advice.

I felt a connection to your character Jing-mei Woo. She and her mother had the same strained relationship that I experienced with my mother. Jing-mei's journey is one I wish to avoid. Jing-mei had a negative relationship with her mother, and once her mother died, she was full of regret and grief. Above all else, I don't want to live life with regrets, so learning Jing-mei's tale made me aware of the mistakes that would later lead to great anguish.

My mother faces the same discrimination you describe in your essay "Mother Tongue" [in the book *The Opposite of Faith: Memories of a Writing Life*]: "People in department stores, at banks, and at restaurants did not take her seriously, did not give her good service, pretended not to understand her, or even acted as if they did not hear her." After rereading this line several times since, it left such a strong impression on me and revealed that I, too, take advantage of my mother. I have discriminated against her without any sympathy merely for her broken English and different ways. However, reading your novel has put my thinking into perspective.

In the sixth grade, I thought the journey of moving from nation to nation was simple, that my mom was the same person in Vietnam as in the U.S., and that the trip was short and clean. But in fact, the experience was complicated and a long process. My mother traveled from Vietnam all the way to the U.S. in order to begin a new life; she integrated into a new culture with a different social and political system. The final straw in her decision to come to the U.S. was that she discovered she was pregnant with me. Now that I've understood this, I've developed a newfound respect for her. She found the courage to change her lifestyle for her children (which is now me and my little brother). She knew that school in Vietnam didn't compare to the educational system in the U.S. (which isn't the best, but still). Suyuan Woo from the novel reminded me of my mother and made me more conscious of the pushes and pulls that lead us to change our life. Suyuan helped me comprehend the struggles my mom faced while making the transition, and how different my life would be if it wasn't for my mother's courage.

Your novel acted as a catalyst in the bond between my

mother and me. I began to meet her halfway in our relationship and put in the extra effort to learn more about her, as well as to speak Vietnamese. Although we still aren't close today and I sometimes take her for granted (still in my rebellious stage), I feel accomplished in understanding her and my culture. When reading *The Joy Luck Club* in sixth grade, I didn't grasp most of the key concepts and themes, but they were the start I needed to understanding the valuable bond between mother and daughter.

Lisa Le

The Giver
Lois Lowry

"I needed to please everyone and have
everyone pleased with me."
Kelsey Bowen

"I believe without a single shadow of a doubt that it is necessary for young people to learn to make choices," Lois Lowry has said. "Learning to make the right choices is the only way they will survive in an increasingly frightening world." Young people who travel to the world of *The Giver* discover, at first, a pleasant place without war or pain, hunger or poverty. In time, however, they discover that sameness, conformity, and a life without choice can carry their own dangers. Lowry's inspiration for the novel grew, in part, from caring for her aging father, who suffered from dementia. She had to tell him about people he had once loved but could no longer name, about events he had experienced but could no longer remember. She began to wonder, What might it be like to live in a world where all painful memories could be erased? Would that be a better world? *The Giver* is her answer.

Dear Lois Lowry,

It feels like there is an entire circus performing in the pit of my stomach. Acrobats, contortionists, and parading animals all flipping and twisting about deep within me, and you, Ms. Lowry, put them there. You led them in one by one and conducted them in this chaotic rampage inside of me, with your book *The Giver* as the ringleader; I have nothing but thanks to offer you.

I am the eldest of two daughters and like most daughters, I love my mother. I do. The problem is that my mother and I do not fit each other. We are the puzzle pieces that look as if they will easily slide together but end up fitting into completely separate spots across the board. I am incurably curious and filled to the brim with wanderlust. I am always craving an adventure, ready to take risks and try new things. I want to experience extraordinary experiences. When I grow old, I want to be exhausted and weak from my youth. I want to milk my health for everything it has and pour it into every crevice of life I can find and have no regrets. My mother, however, is completely the opposite. She is always worried, always fussing with what-ifs. She mutes all chances of danger by extinguishing every flame of life that shows itself to her (and me).

My mother soon became a dark shroud that hung over me. She controlled every aspect of my life: what came into my life, what came out, and even how I dealt with it. Every part of me and the world around me went under scrupulous inspection by my mother; if there was a crack in the sidewalk I was walking on, I could fully depend on my mother knowing exactly how deep and how long it was. When I finally got my driver's license, I thought that her hovering cloud of overprotectiveness would dissolve into a mist of trust and respect. It didn't. It grew darker, heavier. My life became dictated, ruled, ordered, *controlled* by my mother. She ran my life. And I let her. I allowed her to drive her freight train of worry and paranoia over my wishes and ambitions, flattening them into distant and soon-forgotten memories.

My meek manner grew like a tumor inside of me, feasting on the constant docile state in which I was confined. Soon, my mother's feet weren't the only ones walking over me. Without protest, I found myself doing whatever was asked of me, whether I wanted to or not. I needed to please everyone and have everyone pleased with me. I was starved of any genuine friendship.

One night only a few months ago, I was rummaging through my room when I found *The Giver*, an old friend among forgotten relics of my childhood. The pages were yellowed and the smell was old, but it fit so perfectly in my hand. Nostalgic memories of admiration and wonder poured over me as I revisited the story I had once been so familiar with. As I flipped through the aged pages of the book, my eyes stuck to a specific line on page 97: "If everything's the same, then there aren't any choices! I want to wake up in the morning and *decide* things!"

Jonas's words resonated in my head. I wasn't sure why

they struck me so immensely. I didn't understand how necessary it was to *decide* things. But I could hear Jonas yelling the words in the back of my head. It wasn't until I picked the book back up and thoroughly read through it, as I had many times years before, that I understood just how liberating it was to make decisions about myself, for myself. And how absolutely exhilarating it is to be in charge of your own life.

Ms. Lowry, there is an entire circus performing in the pit of my stomach, and it is in the best way possible. I never could have imagined that a children's book set in a dystopia could ever relate to my boring, eventless life. But you have taught me so much — things my mother has been too scared to communicate to me. You have taught me the important lesson of living my own life. You have taught me that to decide is to control. You have taught me that even though I am young, I have a life to live. And most important, you have taught me that you sometimes have to run away from the people who have your best interest in mind. Don't worry: I won't go strutting around my school, dismissing my teachers and cursing my mother. But I am deciding things for myself. Small decisions, such as what I wear to school, and big decisions, such as which universities I'll apply to. So thank you, Ms. Lowry. Thank you, Jonas. Thank you for showing me that deciding on either a blue tunic or a red tunic could lead me to a life of grander decisions.

Truly and freely yours,
Kelsey Bowen

Legend
MARIE LU

"In order to protect ourselves,
we have to hurt our loved ones."
Macoy Churchill

Can a person be good and bad at the same time, both a hero and a villain? Marie Lu thinks so. Her novel *Legend* tells the story of two such characters, teenagers struggling to survive in a futuristic world marked by plague and environmental disasters. Day is a criminal, high on the most-wanted list. And yet among his crimes is breaking into a hospital to steal much-needed medications for his family. June is the prodigy warrior assigned to capture and bring Day to justice. As June learns more about Day's true character, fulfilling her mission becomes increasingly difficult. Marie Lu says she enjoys exploring that gray area where most people live, somewhere between good and evil, between seeking justice and exacting revenge.

Dear Marie Lu,

Being a criminal comes with a certain looming paranoia, even for the craftiest of criminals. You have to plan
out your every move, never missing even the smallest of
details, and if you slip up, the law will not blink an eye at
throwing you into a cell you worked so hard to avoid. Just
like Day, my heart was the very thing that caused me to
end up with undesirable metal cuffs around my wrists and
that led to the foreign sound of a juvenile cell door clicking
closed behind me to become routine. My inability to let my
brother take my possession charges for me made me feel
like Day, bounding from the room of his childhood home
to his imminent capture. My actions metaphorically put
my family, especially my mother, in the direct line of fire.
I read *Legend* and realized that I was stuck, incarcerated,
thinking of the harm my actions had on my family, just like
Day in his cell.

An overwhelming interest started to overtake me when
I started to make connections between my criminal actions
and Day's. I would remember sitting in my car overlook-
ing my house, envisioning my family's actions while they
resided comfortably inside the house. Overtaken by substance, I felt like someone else watching over my family,
like I couldn't go in because of the possible repercussions it
would have on my family. Day knew exactly the same thing
would happen if he entered his childhood home. Although
our situations were different, they were the same. We
watched over our family for comfort, but couldn't be with

them because we were different. The son we once had been was overtaken by a life of crime. Although we wanted the situation to change, we knew it would never be the same.

Day let his heart destroy his flawless criminal history to avoid a simple argument with someone he cared about, and I did the same thing. I was a good criminal, and I knew every step to take to avoid being caught. When I asked my brother if we should take precautions to avoid being caught, he said it would take too much time. I knew what we should do, but to avoid an argument with my brother, I decided to take my chances. Day did a very similar thing. He knew the trouble in saving a stranger, but to avoid the solemn eyes of Tess, he took his chances. We decided to roll the dice to avoid having to look in the eyes of our upset loved ones, and inevitably it was our downfall. Criminals cannot have hearts, or good intentions. In order to protect ourselves, we have to hurt our loved ones. When I gained this knowledge from your book, I felt better as I lay in my cell; I knew that hurting my loved ones wasn't worth a flawless criminal history and so did Day.

The connections I made to *Legend* caused me to lie stunned in my frigid cell. This book taught me lessons about my criminal life when I didn't even take a step. It showed me exactly where my criminal conduct would take me if I refused to see the enclosed walls around me. *Legend* caused me to open my eyes to the inevitable capture of every criminal regardless of his or her wit, effort, and will to avoid incarceration. Unlike Day I don't have an exquisite lover like June to ensure my freedom. My capture is only escaped through the time given by the judicial system. As I flipped the last page, I knew that letting my brother take my charges would be equivalent to John taking Day's place on the firing line. If I were to allow my criminal conse-quences to fall on my family's shoulders, then my loved ones and society would have to suffer.

Only through *Legend* was I able to see this fact. Before I dove into this book, I was blind to the cell I was in, the situation that only I put myself into, and the metaphori-cal massacre of my family's emotions. Through *Legend* I became aware of my profound need to change. For that I could never thank you enough.

Macoy Churchill

The House on Mango Street
SANDRA CISNEROS

"I am not fat anymore. I never was, I suppose."
Julia Mueller

In creating the character of twelve-year-old Esperanza, a girl growing up in a Latino neighborhood in Chicago, Sandra Cisneros tapped into her own childhood memories. Writing about Esperanza and her adventures with her friends Lucy and Rachel was, Cisneros says, "a way of claiming this is who I am." What began as a memoir eventually became the novel *The House on Mango Street*. For the author, the book celebrates her childhood and her culture, "all of the people I loved in the neighborhood I came from."

The story depicts one year in the life of Esperanza, no longer a little girl but not yet a woman. She longs to be grown up but is not quite ready. In one adventure, the friends find a pair of red high-heeled shoes and parade in them down the street. "I remember when I was a young girl," Cisneros says, "how much we wanted those high heels. But we didn't realize all the baggage it brought with it, all the attention, all the men on the corner sending kisses to us and saying things." The friends give up the shoes, not ready yet to be "beautiful."

Dear Sandra Cisneros,

"We are tired of being beautiful."

There was nothing between us until then. You and your book were over my head, or beneath it. Then you hooked me. "We are tired of being beautiful," you wrote in *The House on Mango Street*. I still whisper it in the mirror.

Sandra, I encourage everyone to get at least a little bit fat at some point in their lives. What greater feat is there to surmount than that of loving something you scorn? How normal it feels to look so regularly "wrong." What kinship you feel to those suffering by the hand of visual standards.

"We are tired of being beautiful."

We have made a terrible mistake, Sandra. We associate *fat* with something undesirable and ugly and unnatural and incorrect. Fine, it can be unhealthy and it can be unflattering; I concede. I will argue forever, though, that it is the single most natural thing: it is the human body occupying space in the universe; it is me and more of me filling up the world, like Venus in every Renaissance portrayal, every ancient sculpture of every glorified woman. These women are fat but they are not ugly, because to be *ugly* is to be *unsightly* and to be *fat* is to be *large*.

We went to Paris last year. While we were there, my cousin (who is beautiful and a singer and not fat at all) poked my stomach in jest. I suppose I didn't get the joke and so I cried on our hotel balcony: huge, heaving sobs that roared with the panicked frustration that I could not easily be what seemed so natural to others. One of my deepest regrets in this life of mine is the fact that I cried in Paris. I can't stand to remember the cold concrete balcony beneath me as I hugged my knees to my chest and sobbed with self-disgust — but it wasn't even self-disgust. I liked myself; I just assumed I ought not to. I sobbed with self-confusion. I cannot stand that I let it get to me, least of all in that perfect city on such a perfect day, my family filling up our little hotel room with laughter. . . . I've always hated when people magnify the little things. We are so small already; we cannot feel that big. I was so small already; I could not be that big.

I needed someone to agree with me. Something in me screamed, the way your character Marin screams when the yellow Cadillac crashes. You understand, Sandra, and that amazed me. As I read *The House on Mango Street*, the weight lifted. I learned that there's worse to be had than extra skin. You showed me that everybody is a little wrong: a little fat, a little slow, a little silly. Even after everything — especially after everything — becoming a little bit fat is the best thing that's ever happened to me. It's all in the overcoming. Struggle, struggle, barely make it. As I read on, you wrote that, too. You wrote the words that were written in me, on me, all over me. What a trick, Sandra.

I can't fathom how you bridged the difference. *The House on Mango Street*. The apartment on 195th. Your house and mine. It is something shared, I suppose, that we both have places to live.

"We are tired of being beautiful." My mother is, and

so am I. Esperanza and Marin and Lucy are, too. So must every woman be. Exhausted of rouge and razors. Lipstick and curling irons. Lacquered nails that cannot scratch at the dirt or else be ruined. Rumbling stomachs that cannot be quelled or else expand. I remember when I was thirteen and I thought that my knees as I knelt were too big. Do you think your knees are too big? Do you ever look down when you're kneeling to pray or fold the laundry and think, *Too big?* They are not, Sandra. They are only doing what they've been made for.

"We are tired of being beautiful." Thank you for writing those words. I was thinking them. I felt their unspoken pressure until they broke off your page and got stuck in my heart. That was your trick, I suppose. You wrote what everyone was thinking. You are so far away from me, so different, and still you spoke to me and I understood you. You knew me all along.

I am not fat anymore. I never was, I suppose, or maybe I still am. But I've stopped thinking about it and I am fine. "I am too strong for her to keep me here forever," you wrote. I know that by "her," you meant Mango Street, but I read it as "my body" and "my mind." My heart came back together then, and I have you to thank for that. You didn't tell me how to pull myself back together; you just showed me that I could. I was tired of trying to be somebody else's definition of *beautiful,* and you told me that was okay. Beauty is not in the beholder, but in she who is beheld.

Julia Mueller

Ariel
Sylvia Plath

"You didn't even try."
Abby Swegarden

"It is as if my life were magically run by two electric currents: joyous positive and despairing negative — whichever is running at the moment dominates my life, floods it."

Sylvia Plath was a high achiever. Her first published poem appeared in 1941, when she was just eight years old. By the time she had graduated from high school, her poems had been published in a number of local papers and magazines, and her short story "And Summer Will Not Come Again" had appeared in *Seventeen* magazine. She won national writing contests and a scholarship to Smith College, where she wrote hundreds of poems during the course of her studies. Her mother believed her daughter set high standards for herself and then drove herself to exhaustion in achieving them, fearful of disappointing others.

The person she seems to have disappointed most, however, was herself. While still a student at Smith, Plath attempted suicide by taking sleeping pills. Doctors said she was suffering from nervous exhaustion. Biographers have indicated that Plath may have had manic depression, also called bipolar disorder. At the time, there were no widely used medications that were effective in treating this illness. During the harsh winter of 1963, while her young children slept, she took her own life. Her legacy is her poetry, mirroring her frenetic charge of joy and despair. *Ariel* is a collection of the poems written near the end of her life, when despair seemed to dominate.

Sylvia,

I wish you more happiness than you got out of life. You deserved the best. I wonder if you saw my mom and I reading you when I was younger, and me not understanding a word of it. I wonder if you saw the words swimming in my head as a stupid eleven-year-old. I wonder if you saw me reading your book of poems in the psych ward at Prairie Psychiatric Hospital and wondering how I could've been so blind to your brilliance as a child.

But, what I really wonder, is: How you could even think of belittling yourself as much as you did in your writing, and as much as you did in your life? I believe it takes time to love yourself. But you didn't even try. YOU DIDN'T EVEN TRY. You knew how brilliant the *Ariel* poems were when you were writing them, and what I don't understand is why you didn't bother to stick around to see how much the world could relate to them. I don't understand how you could leave what you worked so hard for in a heap of embarrassment and nothingness. I don't understand how you could know that they were so inspiring and amazing, and not even bother to live out the praise you would've gotten for them. I do not understand that.

But, at the same time, I do. I've been there. I understand what happens and what it feels like when all you want to do is take the knife in the kitchen and open your veins until all you can feel is blood seeping out. I understand that it doesn't matter that the one thing keeping you alive before can do absolutely nothing for you anymore. I understand that you can try so hard to care about something, and it slips through your fingers like silk. I understand how you can't believe in anything anymore, not even the thing that made you famous or that made you love so long ago (even though it was probably just days, even weeks), and I understand how everything can change in a mere second.

So maybe I don't know what I'm trying to say. Maybe this letter is just a letter of selfishness because I still want more. Because I didn't want to see you, an amazing writer and someone who could reach the depths of the darkness of my heart — so easily it hurt to breathe — just disappear like that. Like I did. I didn't know what to do with myself, and you probably didn't, either. But I do remember sitting in the living room and telling my mother I would like to meet you one day, and she told me I couldn't. I asked why, and she said, "Because . . . because, you just can't. She doesn't exist anymore." And I left it at that, because there was nothing else to say. I would listen to my mother read everything from "Daddy" to "Mad Girl's Love Song." (That was my favorite — I would read it over and over again. And what's funny is it's retained its original authenticity in my life and has played a huge part in analyzing every relationship I've ever had. They all fit into that poem. Every one.) And I would fall in love with every word. I couldn't help myself.

So today is a day that I am remembering what you gave me. You helped me to shape my childhood and you helped to shape the person I was last summer, the girl with red arms and tears stained onto every one of her days. You helped me come out of that, and you helped me realize that wishing someone was alive doesn't do anything for you, or for that person. It just makes you long for them. It just makes you miss something that you can't have even more. You, and life in general, taught me that you have to just accept things, like yourself, and just move on. You have to do it in order to simply survive. To live from day to day. You have to realize that no amount of scars on your arms or of Tylenol in your upset stomach is going to make things better. Only you can do that, and only you. You're all you've got.

I'll give you something in closing. I love these lines. And I think, if you were to have survived, you would, too. I wish you great happiness, wherever you are. You mean everything to me . . . sometimes.

It just gets hard to believe
That god sent this angel to watch over me
'Cause my angel
She don't receive my calls
Says I'm too dumb to . . .
Too dumb to fight
Too dumb to save
Well, maybe I don't need no angel at all.

Abby Swegarden

"When Death Comes"
MARY OLIVER

"I am armed with your words."
Aidan Kingwell

"I just begin with these little notebooks and scribbled things as they came to me. And then worked them into poems later," says Mary Oliver. She describes her childhood as "troubled" and says that escaping into nature, walking through the woods with a volume of poetry by Walt Whitman in her knapsack, "saved" her. She found her voice, her place in the world.

Like Walt Whitman, Mary Oliver is a poet and a lover of nature. Her observations of nature — from woodland to salt ponds, from skunk cabbage to fields of flowers — infuse her poetry, and for many young readers, her poems provide a window of understanding about themselves and their world. Her work has been compared to that of her beloved Walt Whitman as well as to that of Henry David Thoreau, another writer who found inspiration in living in harmony with nature.

Dear Mary,

I know it's an unconventional subject for a letter: death. A fact of life that most of us endeavor to avoid, or at least ignore. But I, Mary — I have walked side by side with death all of my life.

I was thirteen the first time I read your poem, and at that time in my life, there was a good chance that I would not see my fourteenth birthday. I had been depressed since age ten, but I had never received any treatment. My mind was very dark; I dove deeper and deeper into my own twisted thoughts with each passing moment. I was someone who was simultaneously terrified of dying and yet obsessed with the idea. I was suicidal, which is a state of being that I cannot well describe, because there are not words that can describe such utter loss of hope, such bitterness and pain and unrelenting sorrow. I wanted to end my own life so badly that most days I could not find one single reason for living. It was not a cry for attention; it was a feeling of utter self-hatred. There is also no accurate way to describe the feeling of hating yourself and your life so much that you long to end it all. It is a feeling of being trapped, of being insane, of being hopeless. When you are suicidal, you are like a wild animal just barely being contained by a thin human shell. Your soul is empty and your heart is blackened and dead. You have no straws left to grasp, no ladder to climb out of the abyss; the only rope offered to help you scramble out is in the shape of a noose, and after weeks or months or years, that noose begins to look very, very appealing.

So there I stood, face-to-face with death on a daily basis, wondering if each new day was the day that it would finally consume me. I was afraid of my own mind. I found no comfort in wooden crosses or the taste of bitter crackers, nor in the deluded words of psychiatrists. That eventual uncertainty — the uncertainty of the terror of my own death — haunted my footsteps as I walked from day to day, wearing it like a heavy, bitter cloak. The very idea of my own death was killing me.

Then, one day, in my seventh-grade English class, I was presented with your poem. My teacher referred to it as "a dark poem with a note of hope underlying it," but within it, I found so much more. Within it, I found new life. My mind opened up as I read your words; I was a frail but inspired butterfly clawing my way from a dark, putrid cocoon. The way you spoke, Mary; the way you talked about death, and how he will come to buy you with "all the bright coins from his purse," how he will come "like an iceberg between the shoulder blades." I could tell: you knew. You knew what it felt like to be owned by death's shadow, in the same way that I was then. You had felt the same terror, the same all-consuming dread. But you were also strong. You faced death and said that it did *not* own you; you had looked into death's dark eyes and said, "No, you cannot have me; I am not yet done here."

When you spoke of not wanting to have simply visited this world, my own world turned upside down. I began to think about how horrible it would be to have only been a visitor, in the way that you said: to not have made my mark on the world, to have only passed through with no real substance. I thought of a life lived entirely in absence of beauty and amazement, a life barren of love or excitement or laughter. I began to realize that that was what suicide would do to me. I saw that life was fast becoming my own. I saw that killing myself would take me away before I even had the chance to make something of my life. Suicide would eliminate my pain, yes, but it would also close any doors of possibility that I might have still open to me, doors that may lead to happiness in my future.

I never would have imagined, Mary, that *not* killing myself would be one of the hardest decisions that I would ever have to make. But in the end, I made the choice, and I am still alive today. My life has not been full of joy; in fact, it has been dark, and hard, and at times I have even slipped back into death's unrelenting grasp. But at those times, I have reminded myself of what I thought then — that I want to make something of my life, and that ending it would mean turning my back on all future possibilities, as well as the few pieces of happiness that I have managed to find in the present. At those dark times, Mary, I often also read your poem to myself — the poem that catalyzed my grand suicidal epiphany. I still struggle with this menace, but now I have one thing that I did not have before: I have hope.

"When Death Comes," Mary — and it will — I want to face it as an equal, and shake its hand as a friend, and accept it as an eventuality. You taught me that that is the only proper way to die. With your words you taught me that life cannot be lived in the shadow of death — that life must be a thing *separate* from death. And you taught me that when death comes, I should embrace it, but also that I should not welcome it before its time. You taught me, Mary, that there was nothing to be feared in death so long as my life was one well lived.

"I don't want to end up simply having visited this world," you wrote.

And "When Death Comes," Mary, I will tell it that you were my friend. Because you were. I will tell it that I am armed with your words, and it will bow its dark face in respect, and then, it will offer me its hand and lead me into whatever may or may not lay behind it. I will feel no fear, Mary — I no longer fear death and all its ways. I will know that I have beaten death down with your words and the inspiration that they gave me. I will know that I did not let it take me in any way but the one I wanted. And I will know that my life, no matter how twisted, corrupt, and fearful, was worth living.

So thank you, Mary. Thank you for wrenching death's grip from my wrist. Thank you for showing me that the burden of my soul was not so dark. That there was still hope left in me.

Aidan Kingwell

The Catcher in the Rye
J. D. SALINGER

"This is a city in need of a Holden Caulfield."
Martha Park

"You never really get the smell of burning flesh out of your nose entirely. No matter how long you live," J. D. Salinger told his daughter years after his experiences in World War II. Salinger had been a writer before he became a soldier. He had conceived of a teenage character named Holden Caulfield. When he was drafted, Salinger took his initial chapters about Holden with him. They stayed with him through the war. And they stayed with him when he checked himself into the hospital, suffering from battle fatigue, a condition that would later be recognized as post-traumatic stress disorder.

As a result of Salinger's war experiences, his understanding of his character Holden changed; as he developed the manuscript, the teenager became more and more disillusioned with the world and deeply disturbed by the death that surrounded him. The resulting novel, *The Catcher in the Rye*, became a touchstone for generations of embittered, depressed, or lonely teenagers.

To J. D. Salinger,

This city needs a soft place to fall as much as I need a soft place to lay my head. These wide streets glitter sadly, beer bottles casting out lonesome rays under the soft glow of streetlights. Down the road a man stumbles out of a bar, howling with laughter as lonely and meaningless as these streets.

I think of you as I walk, cold and clutching a sketchbook and a marker. I think of Holden Caulfield, too, as the lost innocence of this city that bears down on me and that he would understand. Holden to me is a sort of unlikely saint. He is a saint of skinny little roller-skate girls and ducks in winter and corny piano players.

I know he would be sad, too, if he could turn the corner with me and if he could feel this long, cold street shudder as an eight-year-old street kid flips himself around and around, in slow motion, his hands and feet meeting the cobblestone ground with a dull thud on each round. His older brother passes a yellow plastic bucket through the crowd of shivering onlookers.

The small boy twists and turns through the air, his eyes shut tight. As he passes by me, I think I can almost hear him singing, "If a body catch a body coming through the rye."

When the bucket gets around to me, I stuff a few meaningless bills in among the others. They're all I have to show for my stumbling empathy, and I turn my back and continue walking, the concrete pounding with my head as behind me the boy continues to fly through the air. A child who here can never stay a child skips ahead of me down the curb past the dirty graffiti-covered walls that are his hateful education.

This city is dead weight waiting for a transformation. It is heavy, like Allie's left-handed baseball glove covered in poems and Sunny's green dress in the closet. This city is a sad collection of lights and empty laughter in opaque glass bottles on the side of the road. This city is running fast toward the edge of a cliff. This is a city in need of a Holden Caulfield.

If there's one thing I've learned from your words through Holden, it's to be true to who I am. I don't want to be counted in Holden's long list of "phonies," like Ossenburger and Sally Hayes and Robert Ackley. Holden awakened in me a sense of responsibility for these awkwardly crumbling souls and streetlights and sidewalks.

Tonight, turning to look at the walls covered in scrawled angry messages to those retaining a bit of hope, I think of you and your Holden. Uncapping my marker, I look carefully for a space on the wall, and when I find it, I leave my own message: *Holden Caulfield was here.* And he is. He's in me and he's in this city and he's in the healing that must take place here. Thank you for him.

Martha Park

Nineteen Eighty-Four
GEORGE ORWELL

"You were so unspeakably right."
Devi Acharya

"What I saw in Spain, and what I have seen since of the inner workings of left-wing parties, have given me a horror of politics." When George Orwell returned to England after his stint in the Indian Imperial Police, his disillusionment with authority and authoritarian regimes had begun. The Spanish Civil War completed it.

A military dictatorship led by General Francisco Franco, with support from the Nazis in Germany and the Fascists in Italy, had overthrown the democratically elected government of Spain. Orwell volunteered to fight alongside the democratic Republicans. He was badly injured, and the Republicans were badly defeated. Franco brutally ruled Spain for the next several decades.

Orwell's horror of politics infused his fiction. In addition to his political parable *Animal Farm*, he is known for *Nineteen Eighty-Four*, a dystopian novel of a totalitarian future in which even language is manipulated to confuse what is real and true and what is not. *Nineteen Eighty-Four* has become so iconic that real-world totalitarian governments and actions are often termed "Orwellian."

To George Orwell:

You were right, you were right, you were right. I'm sorry I never saw it before, and I feel like an idiot, sitting here and penning this to you when you were so unspeakably right. You shouldn't have published those books of yours under the guise of fiction — how could fiction be what's happening outside my very doorstep? People get so worked up, angry, at some imaginary oppressive tyrant when the very dystopias we fear and loathe are being built around us. I'm only just beginning to see them myself — brick and mortar meant to keep worlds apart, shields of hatred and arrows of intolerance, warlords arming for battle while the unwitting peasants continue to live from day to day. Soon only the fortress, a bastion cutting down any hope of love or compassion, will remain, with every citizen gripped tight in the steely apathy of law.

Oh, if only I could make you understand just how important — how fundamental! — your work has been to my life! If only I knew I would be able to express such a thing in this letter — and it not come across as the ramblings of a madman! What I enumerated before, but feel I have not adequately expressed, is that you were right. I first read *Animal Farm* when I was young — too young to understand it. I thought of it as a humorous fable, nothing more. Every day I saw oppression — in the news, on the street, in my home. Every day I watched as underlings tried to rise above their rulers, getting drunk on power and imposing rule harsher than that of that previous tyrant.

I saw the denizens, mindless and dumb — waiting to see who the new ruler would be, wondering if they should care. And in my wide-eyed youth I did not think, *Those are Orwell's words! Those are the very actions, painted on the canvas of reality! That group is made of pigs, and those other fellows' horses and goats and sheep. Here is where the story starts, and here is where it will end, every word as he penned it.* My eyes might have been as blind as those vacant stares about me, but to my credit, I did observe. I watched people and places and motivations and reactions. I tried to piece my world together through the map you created.

Then came your work *Nineteen Eighty-Four*. This piece was the key that turned the lock in my mind, allowing me to see that this was real, that vigilance was needed. I saw in my slovenly compatriots the face of Parsons, and in my fellow youth those trained only to follow orders and the herd under the guise of "team building" and crafting "character." I saw the posing, the scare tactics, the hype and hysteria. I saw the pain of real terrorism as it happened, and then saw the far more expansive, far more deadly panic and paranoia of imagined threats of terrorism.

Now what do I see when I dare to venture outside my tiny safe haven? Drones circling overhead. Cell phones that track every move, conversations being recorded and analyzed indiscriminately for any sign of suspicion. More and more information has been released, telling evidence of our descent into dystopia — and yet people seem to become ever more complacent! Scandals blow up in a day

and are gone the next. Disaster relief gets attention perhaps for only a few months. People would much rather live
in an era where superheroes and men with guns can solve
all the problems in the world. And I must confess, I can't
blame them for that.

I am not saying, sir, that I think that every aspect of
society is awful and must be usurped, countermanded,
destroyed. I love this world. That's why I want to protect
it. I am saying (as you have said) that people must always
watch the world around them instead of drifting between
obligations and pleasure, as so many do now. That's the
reason I wrote this letter — to say (for it must be reiter-
ated this one last time) that you were right. Right to write
your books, right to do all that you have done to better
the world. I, too, have begun my first steps in the world
of writing, describing the world I see around me just as
you did. I hope to be, just as you have been, an observer
spinning my cautionary tales, trying to help the world
understand. You are truly an inspiration. Your words will
echo in this world for centuries to come.

Good-bye for now,
Devi Acharya

Night
Elie Wiesel

"I consider writing another form of resistance."
Annie Schnitzer

"Auschwitz. The watchtowers. The barbed wire." In his memoir *And the Sea Is Never Full,* Elie Wiesel describes approaching the site of the former concentration camp. At first he writes just single words, punctuated, it seems, by silence. As he walks past what was "his block," the rush of memories engulfs him. In Birkenau, he closes his eyes but can still see what is no longer there: "the thick smoke, the small heaps of ashes."

Elie Wiesel returned to the concentration camps in 1979 as part of a fact-finding mission for President Jimmy Carter's Commission on the Holocaust, thirty-four years after he'd been liberated from Buchenwald and twenty-five years after François Mauriac convinced him to start writing what would become his first memoir, *Night.*

Dear Mr. Wiesel,

I am the granddaughter of Holocaust survivors. My grandfather Abraham Roy was the first person to escape from the Chelmno death camp. My grandmother Taube and grandaunt Frania both endured at Auschwitz. Growing up, they explained the importance of resistance. For my grandmother, resistance meant maintaining her humanity even during times of horror and complete desperation. It is important to preserve one's memories and to ensure that such atrocities are not forgotten. Writing is an expression of survival and continuity. I read your memoir of the death camps, *Night*. Never before had I read such a vivid and powerful account by anyone — it overwhelmed me. I could never imagine the pain and suffering that so many people faced, but reading your story allowed me to connect with my own history at a different level. My respect for my grandparents (and other survivors) has only deepened.

The relationship between you and your father reminded me of my own father; I could not live without him nor could I imagine losing him. I realized that the Nazis' systematic dehumanization sometimes caused people to turn against each other. Just reading about the pain and death made my heart break. Your book allowed me to look at my own life and reevaluate what is truly important. These are the thoughts that accompanied me last summer as I traveled to Poland to visit the concentration camps, Chelmno and Auschwitz, where my grandparents were imprisoned and where most of my family perished.

Chelmno was the first Nazi extermination camp and was the model for later death camps. It was there that approximately 150,000 people were murdered and only seven survived. My family and I went there to lay a plaque in memory of my grandfather and the other members of my family who were murdered at Chelmno. The plaque is mounted on a memorial wall near several mass graves as a tribute to those who perished. One side of the wall is dedicated to those people who died in the camp while the other side is meant for those who survived; we were the first to lay a plaque of remembrance.

I remember standing in the fields, looking at the mass graves. The place seemed so peaceful and quiet; the trees were gently swaying in the wind. It seemed so incongruous with the unspeakable crimes committed there. I walked the dirt road taken by trucks that transported dead bodies to the mass graves. I tried to imagine this terrible scene but found it incomprehensible.

After Chelmno, we visited Auschwitz-Birkenau. For me this was the hardest part of the trip because of the searing images that were imprinted in my mind by your book. We visited the primitive barracks where my grandparents slept. Your descriptions of the living conditions and my seeing them gave me a powerful sense of how extreme the experience must have been. The walls in the barracks contained colorful murals of children going to *shul* (school). Here in the midst of all this pain, there was still creation, yet it was mournful and sad. Afterward, I walked outside and stood in front of the train tracks that brought people to their death. The path next to the tracks was covered with stones that were worn flat by the one million people who walked over them.

Your personal story, Mr. Wiesel, combined with my own journey to Poland, helped me think more about my own identity as a Jew. It made me realize that I am proud to be Jewish especially because of my background. I am proud of my grandparents who showed courage and strength in the face of unimaginable terror. I speak up for what I believe in not only because I am Jewish but because it is the right thing to do. My grandmother spoke out against injustice and refused to remain silent. She taught this lesson to my mother who taught it to me. Your story has given me a way to connect with a family history that I have not lived but that is a part of me. You have helped me deepen my understanding, and I thank you for it.

Annie Schnitzer

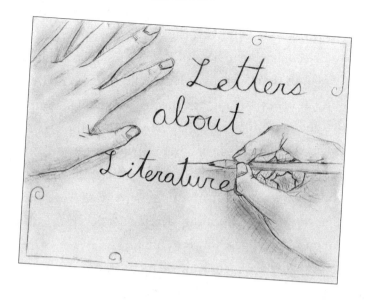

Letters About Literature began in the 1980s as Books Change Lives, a reading promotion program of the Center for the Book in the Library of Congress. In 1992, with the sponsorship of *Weekly Reader*, the program evolved into an essay contest for young readers using the letter format. At a time when the Internet was increasing in popularity and e-mail was replacing snail mail, launching a program that required students to actually pen or type their letters and then mail them might have seemed counterintuitive. Yet participation in the program soared from four thousand letters in its first year to more than ten thousand in its second. Over the years, with national funding from Target, the Library of Congress James Madison Council, and most recently, Dollar General Literacy Foundation, the annual number of entries from young readers has exceeded fifty thousand.

Teachers, in particular, have valued the program's reflective writing approach. Each year, hundreds of teachers submit letters of their own, sharing with the Center for the Book how the program has changed the lives of their students and taken them to new places in their writing. Many children who do not necessarily shine at other writing assignments take ownership of this particular challenge of writing a letter to an author. They write about themselves in a conversational way, often revealing personal details. Many teachers have written that they have learned more about their students from this activity than from any other.

When we began compiling the letters for this collection, we faced the somewhat daunting but pleasant task of tracking down our winning essayists from years past. Our LAL "alumni," as it turns out, include quite a few teachers, editors, some writers — as well as young people who have chosen to follow careers unrelated to teaching or publishing. Without exception, when we contacted them, they remembered the program and the genuine feeling of accomplishment in having received state or national recognition.

"I've never gotten to adequately express my gratitude for everything that the Letters About Literature contest meant to me, and all the ways it's affected me since then," Martha Park, now a freelance writer and editor, wrote to us. *Journeys* expresses *our* gratitude to the hundreds of thousands of young readers and teachers who participated in the Letters About Literature program.

• ABOUT THE CENTER FOR THE BOOK •

The Library of Congress Center for the Book, which includes the Young Readers Center and Poetry and Literature Center, promotes books and libraries, literacy and reading, and poetry and literature. Established by public law in 1977, the Center for the Book incorporates several public-private partnerships designed to implement programs, awards, and prizes in order to nurture and expand a culture of literacy and reading. The Center has affiliates in all fifty states, the District of Columbia, and the U.S. Virgin Islands, and maintains reading and literacy promotion partnerships with more than eighty organizations in the United States and abroad. As a part of the new National and International Outreach division within the Library of Congress, it is the mission of the Center for the Book to nurture and empower this network of organizations in order to strengthen its capacity to serve communities and to provide the broadest access to the vast, diverse, and rich collections of the Library of Congress.

Center for the Book programs include the National Book Festival and the Books & Beyond author series, in which writers from across the country come to the Library to discuss their work and their use of the Library's extraordinary resources.

The Center places special emphasis on young readers through reading and writing contests, the Read.gov website, and the new Young Readers Center in the Thomas Jefferson Building on Capitol Hill.

• Source Notes •

Foreword

p. xi: "I cannot live without books": Thomas Jefferson to John Adams, June 10, 1815, in Lester J. Cappon, ed., The Adams-Jefferson Letters, Chapel Hill, NC: University of North Carolina Press, 1959 (reprint 1988), p. 243.

Chapter One

p. 3: "These times are too . . . depend on 'em": Wilder, p. 192.

p. 11: "Good historical fiction . . . over the head with it": Blasingame, p. 38.

p. 11: "fact and incident": ibid.

p. 13: "an hallucination": quoted in Parini, p. 212.

Chapter Two

p. 15: "I have dared to do strange things — bold things": quoted in "Emily Dickinson."

p. 17: "I'm Nobody! Who are you?" and "They'd banish us, you know.": Dickinson, p. 279.

p. 18: "I learned to dream through reading": Draper, "Welcome!"

p. 21: "accuracy of fact . . . spirit": Draper, "*Out of My Mind*: Intro, Summary, and General Questions."

p. 26: "When I write I can shake off all my cares": Frank, p. 251.

p. 26: "I've reached the point . . . change events anyway": ibid., p. 184.

p. 29: "To my vanilla ... chocolate": Pinkney, copyright and dedication page.

p. 30: "I am black. I am unique," "I am the creamy ... ice cream," and "I am ... in a cookie": ibid., passim.

p. 32: "primitive," "off the beaten path," "mysterious swamps," and "great live oaks ... Spanish moss": quoted in Lillios.

p. 32: "urban confusion": quoted in Cort, p. 269.

p. 35: "Not only was I the new kid ... and was chubby" and "This was especially ... about animals": quoted in Sutherland.

p. 35: "secret heroes": Doty, p. 14.

pp. 37–38: "Maybe we should be ... not completely": ibid., p. 48.

p. 39: "I'm an adult ... stuck at thirteen," "That's when things clicked for me," and "As a writer ... uncomfortable situations": Van Draanen.

p. 43: An editor at Simon and Schuster ...: William Cole, "About Alice, a Rabbit, a Tree ...; ... and a Book about Me," *New York Times Book Review*, September 9, 1973.

p. 43: "good books for bad children": quoted in Nordstrom, p. xviii.

p. 45: "and everyone hugs instead of tugs": Silverstein, p. 19.

Chapter Three

p. 46: "Nature brings us fully alive": Calhoun.

p. 48: "spent many hours ... in our basement": quoted in "Carl Hiaasen."

p. 51: "I think I had something ... school system" and "And without talking ... as well as at home": quoted in Harper.

p. 54: "Today is gone. ... another one": Seuss, p. 63.

p. 55: "Even as a child ... doing what was right" and "My parents have always ... rubbed off on me": quoted in Borné.

p. 58: "Peer pressure . . . Permission to be oneself": quoted in Lodge.

Chapter Four

p. 63: "Since every air raid . . . Light and the Dark": Cooper.

p. 66: "What I feared most . . . not poverty, but failure": Rowling.

pp. 66–67: "grim," "grinding poverty," and "the evils humankind . . . ever known before": quoted in Parker.

p. 71: "Looking back . . . humbug generally": Orwell, p. 7.

p. 71: "the dirty work . . . flogged with bamboos": ibid., p. 236.

p. 75: "She was bright . . . T-ball team": Paterson, *Stories*, p. 250.

p. 75: "the fatal chapter": ibid., p. 251.

p. 75: Was this a story . . . Friendship: ibid., p. 252.

Chapter Five

p. 81: "musings of a thirteen-year-old schoolgirl": Frank, p. 6.

p. 81: "When I write . . . revived!": ibid., p. 251.

p. 83: "I tried first person . . . what I wanted": quoted in Stillman.

p. 87: "It's not like I want . . . can be in public" and "so be it": quoted in Chrisafis.

p. 91: "I had discovered . . . to another" and "Anyone who moved . . . in the head": quoted in "Nobel Prize in Literature 1983."

p. 95: "I wasn't worried about freedom" and "*Fahrenheit* is not . . . bombardment of factoids": "Bradbury on Censorship/Television."

p. 97: "Colored people don't like . . . Burn the book": Bradbury, *Fahrenheit*, p. 89.

p. 97: "Is it true . . . start them?": ibid., p. 38.

p. 97: "Do you ever *read* . . . you burn?": ibid., p. 37.

p. 97: "Are you happy?": ibid., p. 39.

p. 98: "It was a pleasure to burn": ibid., p. 33.

p. 100: "Literature is a fantastic . . . your own challenges": quoted in Jensen.

p. 100: "a cautionary tale": ibid.

p. 104: "from science . . . to journalism": Isaacson, *Benjamin Franklin*, p. 20.

p. 104: "he tried to picture . . . light beam": Isaacson, *Einstein*, p. 3.

p. 104: "imaginative leaps" and "like a pathfinder . . . what lay ahead": Isaacson, *Steve Jobs*, p. 566.

p. 107: "nothing succeeds like excess": Oscar Wilde, "A Woman of No Importance," *The Plays of Oscar Wilde*, vol. 1, Boston: Luce, 1905, p. 63.

Chapter Six

p. 108: "In a hole . . . lived a hobbit": Tolkien, *Hobbit*, p. 1.

p. 108: "Hobbits are just . . . or latent power" and "the stories were made . . . for the languages": quoted in Collier.

p. 113: "When Mr. Bilbo Baggins . . . in Hobbiton": Tolkien, *Fellowship*, p. 21.

p. 117: "I want to do . . . talent God gave me" and "I hope . . . better and better": quoted in Singh.

p. 121: "I swore never to . . . humiliation" and "We must take . . . never the tormented": Wiesel, Nobel Acceptance Speech.

p. 126: "No one reaches out . . . will understand" and "And I've heard over . . . people felt understood": Diaz.

Chapter Seven

p. 133: "I was impressed with it because . . . grasp and call mine": Wallis, p. xii.

p. 135: "Let us die trying": ibid., p. 16.

p. 136: "condemned to die": ibid., p. 14.

p. 137: "I was probably eight . . . I was writing": "Khaled Hosseini Interview."

p. 141: "a way to be good again": Hosseini, p. 2.

p. 142: "I don't love to . . . they surprise me": quoted in Haupt.

Chapter Eight

p. 147: "I come from a family . . . doomed by them": quoted in Fineman.

p. 151: "My duty was . . . defending them": quoted in Guibert.

p. 154: "I hate you . . . love for you" and "I do not see . . . you blindly": Neruda, p. 914.

p. 155: "I was a coward. I went to war": O'Brien.

p. 156: "war stories aren't always . . . the human heart" and "a bad childhood . . . they're carrying": ibid.

p. 160: "Words are . . . used by mankind": quoted in "Rudyard Kipling Biography."

p. 162: "If you can keep . . . a Man, my son": Kipling, p. 170.

p. 164: "It became apparent . . . Saudi royalty!": Abdel-Fattah.

p. 168: "entire life savings," "There was a little . . . could be lucrative," and "make a dime": "Amy Tan Interview."

p. 172: "turning point" and "I couldn't have . . . geography": ibid.

p. 176: "I believe without . . . to make choices" and "Learning to make . . . increasingly frightening world": Lowry, "In Their Own Words."

p. 178: "If everything's the same . . . and *decide* things!": Lowry, *The Giver*, p. 97.

Chapter Nine

p. 184: "a way of claiming this is who I am," "all of the people . . . I came from," and "I remember when . . . saying things": Montagne.

p. 185: "We are tired of being beautiful": Cisneros, p. 42.

p. 187: "I am too strong . . . forever": ibid., p. 110.

p. 188: "It is as if my life . . . floods it": quoted in "Sylvia Plath, 1932–1963."

p. 193: "I just began with . . . into poems later": Tippet.

p. 195: "all the bright coins from his purse" and "like an iceberg between the shoulder blades": Oliver, p. 10.

p. 197: "I don't want . . . visited this world": ibid., p. 11.

p. 198: "You never really get . . . long you live": quoted in Rosenbaum.

p. 199: "If a body catch . . the rye": Salinger, p. 150.

p. 201: "What I saw in Spain . . . horror of politics": quoted in Leys.

p. 205: "Auschwitz . . . barbed wire" and "the thick smoke . . . ashes": Wiesel, *Sea*, pp. 191 and 192.

• BIBLIOGRAPHY •

Abdel-Fattah, Randa. "Interview with Me." Randa Abdel-Fattah website. http://www.randaabdelfattah.com/interview-randa-abdelfattah.asp.

"Amy Tan Interview." Academy of Achievement website, June 28, 1996. http://www.achievement.org/autodoc/page/tan0int-1#.

Blasingame, Jim. "An Interview with Avi, 2003 Newbery Medal Winner for *Crispin, The Cross of Lead*." *ALAN Review* 30, no. 3 (Spring/Summer 2003): 38–39. http://scholar.lib.vt.edu/ejournals /ALAN/v30n3/pdf/blasingame1.pdf.

Bleau, N. Arthur. "Robert Frost's Favorite Poem." In *Frost: Centennial Essays*, edited by Jac Tharpe. Jackson, MI: University Press of Mississippi, 1978.

Borné, Eliza. "Kristin Levine: The Power of Friendship and Quiet Strength." *BookPage* website, February 13, 2012. http://bookpage.com/interviews/8789-kristin-levine#.VmnivXarS70.

"Bradbury on Censorship/Television." Ray Bradbury website. April 2001. http://www.raybradbury.com/at_home_clips.html.

Bradbury, Ray. *Fahrenheit 451*. New York: Ballantine, 1953.

———. *Zen in the Art of Writing*. New York: Bantam, 1990.

Calhoun, Dia. "Wonder and Refuge: My Lifelong Passion for Children's Literature." Dia Calhoun blog. http://diacalhoun.blogspot.com/p /bio.html.

"Carl Hiaasen." *Encyclopedia of World Biography*. www.notablebiographies.com.

Chrisafis, Angelique. "The Curse of the Five-Thousand-Pound Mouse." *The Guardian*, June 10, 2009. www.theguardian.com/books/2009 /jun/11/art-spiegelman-maus-comic-sketchbooks.

Cisneros, Sandra. *The House on Mango Street*. New York: Vintage, 1991.

Collier, Pieter. "1971 BBC radio interview with J. R. R. Tolkien." Tolkien Library website. http://www.tolkienlibrary.com/press/804 -Tolkien-1971-BBC-Interview.php.

Cooper, Susan. "Interview." The Lost Land of Susan Cooper website. http://www.thelostland.com/about/interview.html.

Cort, Carol. *A to Z of American Women Writers*. New York: Infobase, 2007.

Diaz, Shelley. "Raw Honesty: Author Jay Asher Talks to *SLJ* About *Thirteen Reasons Why*." *School Library Journal*, February 27, 2014. http://www.slj.com/2014/02/interviews/raw-honesty-author-jay -asher-talks-to-slj-about-thirteen-reasons-why/#_.

Dickinson, Emily. *The Poems of Emily Dickinson*. Edited by R. W. Franklin. Variorum edition. Cambridge, MA: Belknap Press/ Harvard University Press, 1998.

Doty, Mark. *Dog Years: A Memoir*. New York: Harper Perennial, 2008.

Draper, Sharon M. "*Out of My Mind*: Intro, Summary, and General Questions." Sharon Draper website. http://sharondraper.com /bookdetail.asp?id=35.

———. "Welcome!" Sharon Draper website. http://sharondraper.com.

"Emily Dickinson." Poetry Foundation website. www.poetryfoundation .org/bio/emily-dickinson.

Fineman, Kelly. "Laura Ruby — an SBBT Interview." *Writing and Ruminating* blog, June 18, 2007. http://kellyrfineman.blogspot.com /2007/06/laura-ruby-sbbt-interview.html.

Frank, Anne. *The Diary of a Young Girl: The Definitive Edition.* Edited by Otto H. Frank and Mirjam Pressler. Translated by Susan Massotty. New York: Doubleday, 1995. Originally published 1952 by Modern Library.

Graff, Lisa. "Character Connections: Finding Yourself in the Story." *Literacy Daily* (International Literacy Association blog), October 18, 2012. http://www.literacyworldwide.org/blog /literacy-daily/2012/10/18/character-connections-finding -yourself-in-the-story-.

Guibert, Rita. "Pablo Neruda, The Art of Poetry No. 14." *Paris Review* 51 (Spring 1971). Translated by Ronald Christ. www.theparisreview. org/interviews/4091/the-art-of-poetry-no-14-pablo-neruda.

Harper, Hilliard. "The Private World of Dr. Seuss: A Visit to Theodor Geisel's La Jolla Mountaintop." *Los Angeles Times,* May 25, 1986. articles.latimes.com/1986-05-25/magazine/tm-7029_1_la-jolla.

Haupt, Jennifer. "Author Interview: Wally Lamb." *Spirituality and Health,* November/December 2013. spiritualityhealth.com/articles /author-interview-wally-lamb.

Hosseini, Khaled. *The Kite Runner.* New York: Riverhead, 2003.

"Interview with Jhumpa Lahiri." BookBrowse website. www.bookbrowse .com/author_interviews/full/index.cfm/author_number/929 /jhumpa-lahiri.

"Interview with Wendelin Van Draanen." *Author* magazine. http://www .authormagazine.org/interviews/interview_page_vandraanen.htm.

Isaacson, Walter. *Benjamin Franklin: An American Life.* New York: Simon and Schuster, 2003.

———. *Einstein: His Life and Universe.* New York: Simon and Schuster, 2008.

———. *Steve Jobs.* New York: Simon and Schuster, 2011.

Jensen, Kelly. "Fifteen Years of *Speak:* An Interview with Laurie Halse Anderson." *Book Riot,* April 8, 2014. http://bookriot.com /2014/04/08/15-years-speak-interview-laurie-halse-anderson/.

"Khaled Hosseini Interview: Afghanistan's Tumultuous History." Academy of Achievement website, July 3, 2008. http://www.achievement.org/autodoc/page/hos0int-1.

Kipling, Rudyard. *Kipling: Poems.* New York: Knopf, 2007.

Leys, Simon. "The Intimate Orwell." *New York Review of Books,* May 26, 2011. http://www.nybooks.com/articles/archives/2011/may/26 /intimate-orwell/.

Lillios, Anna. "Rawlings's Life." From *Crossing the Creek: The Literary Friendship of Zora Neale Hurston and Marjorie Kinnan Rawlings* (Gainesville: University Press of Florida, 2010). Marjorie Kinnan Rawlings Society website. http://rawlingssociety.org/rawlings-bio.

Lodge, Sally. "Children's Bookshelf Talks with Jerry Spinelli." *Publishers Weekly,* June 7, 2007. http://www.publishersweekly.com/pw /by-topic/authors/interviews/article/13877-children-s-bookshelf -talks-with-jerry-spinelli.html.

Lowry, Lois. *The Giver.* Boston: Houghton Mifflin, 1993.

———. "In Their Own Words: Authors Talk About Censorship." Random House website. http://www.randomhouse.com/teens /firstamendment/authors.html#lowry.

Lu, Marie. *Legend.* New York: Putnam, 2011.

Montagne, Renee. "*House on Mango Street* Celebrates Twenty-Five Years." National Public Radio, *Morning Edition,* April 9, 2009. http://www.npr.org/templates/story/story.php?storyId =102900929.

Neruda, Pablo. *The Poetry of Pablo Neruda.* New York: Farrar, Straus and Giroux, 2005.

"Nobel Prize in Literature 1983: William Golding." Swedish Academy press release, October 1983. http://www.nobelprize.org/nobel _prizes/literature/laureates/1983/press.html.

Nordstrom, Ursula. *Dear Genius: The Letters of Ursula Nordstrom*. Edited by Leonard S. Marcus. New York: HarperCollins, 1998.

O'Brien, Tim. "President's Lecture." Writing Vietnam Conference, Brown University, April 21, 1999. http://cds.library.brown.edu/projects /WritingVietnam/obrien.html.

Oliver, Mary. *New and Selected Poems*. Boston: Beacon, 1992.

Orwell, George. *An Age Like This, 1920–1940*. Vol. 1 of *The Collected Essays, Journalism, and Letters of George Orwell*. Boston: Godine, 2000. Originally published 1968 by Harcourt, Brace.

Parini, Jay. *Robert Frost: A Life*. New York, Henry Holt, 1999.

Parker, Ian. "Mugglemarch: J. K. Rowling Writes a Realist Novel for Adults." *New Yorker*, October 1, 2012. http://www.newyorker .com/magazine/2012/10/01/mugglemarch.

Paterson, Katherine. "Are You There, God?" Cambridge Forum speech, November 18, 2004. National Children's Book and Literacy Alliance website. http://thencbla.org/education/speeches/are-you-there-god/.

———. *Stories of My Life*. New York: Dial, 2014.

Pinkney, Sandra L. *Shades of Black: A Celebration of Our Children*. Photographs by Myles Pinkney. New York: Scholastic, 2000.

Rawlings, Marjorie Kinnan. *Cross Creek*. New York: Collier, 1987. Originally published 1942 by Scribner's.

Rosenbaum, Ron. "The Flight from Fortress Salinger." Review of *Dream Catcher: A Memoir*, by Margaret A. Salinger. *New York Times*, October 8, 2000. http://www.nytimes.com/books/00/10/08 /reviews/001008.08rosenbt.html.

Rowling, J. K. "The Fringe Benefits of Failure, and the Importance of Imagination." *Harvard Magazine*, June 5, 2009. http://harvardmagazine.com/2008/06/the-fringe-benefits -failure-the-importance-imagination.

"Rudyard Kipling Biography." Biography.com. http://www.biography.com/people/rudyard-kipling-9365581.

Salinger, J. D. *The Catcher in the Rye*. Boston: Little, Brown, 1951.

Seuss, Dr. *One Fish, Two Fish, Red Fish, Blue Fish*. New York: Beginner Books, 1960.

Silverstein, Shel. *Where the Sidewalk Ends*. New York: Harper and Row, 1974.

Singh, Anita. "Harper Lee to Disclose Why She Stopped Writing after *To Kill a Mockingbird*." *The Telegraph*, April 27, 2011. http://www .telegraph.co.uk/culture/culturenews/8463233/Harper-Lee-to -disclose-why-she-stopped-writing-after-To-Kill-A-Mockingbird .html.

Stillman, Heidi. "Interview with Markus Zusak." Chicago Public Library website, spring 2012. www.chipublib.org/interview-with-markus -zusak/.

Sutherland, Amy. "Mark Doty: Poet and Biography Buff." *Boston Globe*, January 6, 2013. http://www.bostonglobe.com/arts/books /2013/01/06/mark-doty-poet-and-biography-buff/ SrjjZxWSrXH9RlZoksqGmM/story.html.

"Sylvia Plath, 1932–1963." Poetry Foundation website. www.poetryfoundation.org/bio/sylvia-plath.

Tippett, Krista. "Mary Oliver — Listening to the World." *On Being*, February 5, 2015. http://www.onbeing.org/program/mary -oliver-listening-to-the-world/transcript/8051#main_content.

Tolkien, J. R. R. *The Fellowship of the Ring*. Boston: Houghton Mifflin, 2001.

———. *The Hobbit*. Boston: Houghton Mifflin, 1966.

Wallis, Velma. *Two Old Women: An Alaska Legend of Betrayal, Courage, and Survival*. Tenth anniversary ed. New York: Harper Perennial, 2004.

Wiesel, Elie. *And the Sea Is Never Full*. New York: Schocken, 2000.

———. Nobel Acceptance Speech, December 10, 1986. Elie Wiesel Foundation for Humanity website. http://www.eliewieselfoundation.org/nobelprizespeech.aspx.

Wilder, Laura Ingalls. *The Long Winter*. New York: HarperCollins, 1981. Originally published 1940 by Harper.

• INDEX •

Abbott, Tony, 8–10
Abdel-Fattah, Randa, 164–167
Acharya, Devi, 201–204
Afghanistan, 137–141
Amnesty International, 67
Anderson, Laurie Halse, 100–103
And the Sea Is Never Full, 205
Animal Farm, 71–74, 201, 202
Ariel, 188–192
Asher, Jay, 126–129
Atefat-Peckham, Darius, 35–38
Athabascans, 133
Audrey, 137–141
Avi, 11–12

Ball, Ellie, 113–116
Beaver, Abbie, 71–74
Blasingame, Jim, 11
Book Thief, The, 83–86
Bowen, Kelsey, 176–179
Bradbury, Ray, 39, 95–99
Bridge to Terabithia, 75–78, 97
Brown, Chelsea, 29–31

Calhoun, Dia, 46–47
Carter, Jimmy, 205
Catcher in the Rye, The, 198–200
Chambers, Elizabeth, 108–112
Chinn, Shannon, 95–99
Choi, Jisoo, 79–82
Churchill, Macoy, 180–183
Cienki, Thomas J., 11–12
Cisneros, Sandra, 184–188
Citizens for Santa Rosa Library, 168

Cole, John Y., xi–xii
Cooper, Susan, 63–65
Crispin: The Cross of Lead, 11–12

Dandelion Wine, 39
DesChamp, Hannah, 151–154
Diary of a Young Girl, The, 26–28, 72, 79–82
Dickinson, Emily, 15–17
Does My Head Look Big in This?, 164–167
Dog Years, 35–38
Dollar General Literacy Foundation, 209
Doty, Mark, 35–38
Draper, Sharon, 18–25
Draughn, Taaja Immani, 18–20
Dyal, Lucy, 1

Eritrea, 4–7
Eva of the Farm, 46–47

Fahrenheit 451, 95–99
Ferris, Gabriel, 104–107
Fire to Fire, 35
Firegirl, 8–10
Forged by Fire, 18–20
Frank, Anne, 26–28, 72, 79–82
Frank, Otto, 26, 79–80
Frost, Robert, 13–14

Gies, Miep, 79–80
Giver, The, 1, 176–179
Giving Tree, The, 43
Glidden, Lacie Craven, 32–34
Golding, William, 61, 91–94

Gorman, Juliana, 121–125
Goyette, Emmy, 100–103
Griffith, Sarah, 131

Haley, Alex, 18
Harry Potter and the Sorcerer's Stone, 66
Harry Potter series, 66–70, 97
Hiaasen, Carl, 48–50
Hobbit, The, 108–112
Hocking, Amanda, 131
Hoff, Jonathan, 87–90
Holocaust, 26–27, 79–90, 121–125, 205–208
Hoot, 48–50
Hosseini, Khaled, 137–141
Houghton Mifflin, 51
House on Mango Street, The, 184–188
"Hug o' War", 43–45

"I'm Nobody! Who are You?", 15–17
"If", 160–163
Indian Imperial Police, 71, 201
Isaacson, Walter, 104–107

Jobs, Steve, 104–107
Joy Luck Club, The, 168–175

Kahn, Eliana, 26–28
Kelly, Aleema, 55–57
Khan, Rahim, 141
King, Martin Luther, Jr., 56, 72
Kingwell, Aidan, 193–197
Kipling, John, 160

Kipling, Rudyard, 160–163
Kite Runner, The, 137–141
Klimek, Davis, 48–50
Kudrin, Bertina, 83–86

Lamb, Wally, 142–146
Langan, Erica, 15–17
Le, Lisa, 172–175
Lee, Hanna, 8–10
Lee, Harper, 117–120
Legend, 180–183
Lentfer, Linnea Rain, 46–47
Levine, Kristin, 55–57
Lions of Little Rock, The, 55–57
Long Winter, The, 2–7
Lord of the Flies, 61, 91–94
Lord of the Rings, The, 113–116
Lowry, Lois, 1, 176–179
Lu, Marie, 180–183

Martin, Katja Saana Sinikka, 13–14
Mauriac, François, 121–122, 205
Maus, 87–90
McLaughlin, Alexandra, 155–159
Middle Ages, 11–12
Miller, Becky, 51–54
Moosman, Arielle, 75–78
Moritz, Kara S., 61, 91–94
Mueller, Julia, 184–187
Mytko, Anna, 43–45

Neruda, Pablo, 151–154
Night, 121–125, 205–208
Nineteen Eighty-Four, 201–204

O'Brien, Tim, 155–159
Oliver, Mary, 193–197
One Fish, Two Fish, Red Fish, Blue Fish, 51–54
Opposite of Faith: Memories of a Writing Life, The, 173

Orwell, George, 71–74, 201–204
Out of My Mind, 21–25
Over Sea, Under Stone, 63–65
Overton, Anne, 66–70

Park, Martha, 198–200
Paterson, Katherine, 75–78
Pinkney, Sandra L., 29–31
Plath, Sylvia, 188–192

Rawlings, Marjorie Kinnan, 32–34
Rowling, J. K., 63, 66–70
Ruby, Laura, 147–150
Running Dream, The, 39–42

Salinger, J. D., 198–200
Sanzhikov, Gerel, 39–42
Schiff, Hillary V., 58–60
Schnitzer, Annie, 205–208
Sclafani, Gabrielle, 142–146
Selassie, Alessandra, 3–7
September 11, 2001, attacks, 139–141
Seuss, Dr., 51–54
Shades of Black, 29–31
She's Come Undone, 142–146
Silverstein, Shel, 43–45
Snow, Janet Lynne, 63–65
"Sonnet LXVI", 151–154
Speak, 100–103
Spiegelman, Art, 87–90
Spinelli, Jerry, 58–60
Stargirl, 58–60
Steve Jobs, 104–107
"Stopping by Woods on a Snowy Evening", 13–14
Stump, Bailee, 126–129
Swegarden, Abby, 188–192
Switched, 131

Tan, Amy, 168–175
Things They Carried, The, 155–159
Thirteen Reasons Why, 126–129
Tiprigan, Joshua, 160–163
To Kill a Mockingbird, 96, 117–120
Tolkien, Christopher, 108
Tolkien, J. R. R., 108–116
Torres, Xiomara, 164–167
Two Old Women, 133–136

Uppaluri, Jayanth, 21–25
Usmani, Ayesha, 168–171

Van Draanen, Wendelin, 39–42
Veglahn, Margaret, 117–120
Vietnam War, 155–159

Wall and the Wing, The, 148–150
Waller, Emily, 147–150
Wallis, Velma, 133–136
"When Death Comes", 193–197
Wichorek, Anna Marie, 133–136
Wiesel, Elie, 121–125, 205–208
Wilder, Laura Ingalls, 2–7
World War I, 160
World War II, 26–27, 63, 79–91, 121–122, 155, 198, 201, 205–208

Yearling, The, 32–34

Zusak, Markus, 83–86